全国职业技能英语系列教材

总主编　童敬东
总顾问　陆松岩

职场
综合英语
实训手册

主　编　童敬东
副主编　董　岩　谢云兰

第一册
（第二版）

Vocational
Comprehensive
English-Training
Course

北京大学出版社
PEKING UNIVERSITY PRESS

图书在版编目(CIP)数据

职场综合英语实训手册.第一册/童敬东主编.—2版.—北京：北京大学出版社，2017.9
（全国职业技能英语系列教材）
ISBN 978-7-301-28593-0

Ⅰ.①职⋯ Ⅱ.①童⋯ Ⅲ.①英语—高等职业教育—习题集 Ⅳ.①H319.6

中国版本图书馆CIP数据核字(2017)第195802号

书　　　名	职场综合英语实训手册　第一册　（第二版）
	ZHICHANG ZONGHE YINGYU SHIXUN SHOUCE DI-YI CE
著作责任者	童敬东　主编
责 任 编 辑	郝妮娜
标 准 书 号	ISBN 978-7-301-28593-0
出 版 发 行	北京大学出版社
地　　　址	北京市海淀区成府路205号　100871
网　　　址	http://www.pup.cn　新浪微博：@北京大学出版社
电 子 信 箱	bdhnn2011@126.com
电　　　话	邮购部 62752015　发行部 62750672　编辑部 62759634
印 刷 者	北京鑫海金澳胶印有限公司
经 销 者	新华书店
	787毫米×1092毫米　16开本　7.75印张　265千字
	2012年8月第1版
	2017年9月第2版　2020年1月第2次印刷
定　　　价	26.00元

未经许可，不得以任何方式复制或抄袭本书之部分或全部内容。
版权所有，侵权必究
举报电话：010-62752024　电子信箱：fd@pup.pku.edu.cn
图书如有印装质量问题，请与出版部联系，电话：010-62756370

第二版前言

《职场综合英语实训手册》是《职场综合英语教程》的配套用书。本书第一版在编写的时候，既照顾了主教材《职场综合英语教程》的单元主题，也参考了英语应用能力考试(B级)的试卷形式，为学习者进一步掌握主教材内容和准备英语应用能力考试提供了必要的资料。然而，第一版面世以来已经过去了五个春秋，高职高专的生源已经悄然发生了变化，英语应用能力考试也于2014年换了新的考试大纲。在此形势下，对原书进行修订，使之与时俱进，更好地服务于高职高专英语教学的需要就成了我们的共识。

在北京大学出版社的大力支持下，原书主编对第一版《职场综合英语教程》及其配套用书从形式到内容进行了研讨，并在此基础上统一了修改意见。《职场综合英语实训手册》的修订工作仍然由各分册主编负责，参加修订的编者还是原班人马。如此分工既能保证本套教材内容的延续性，又能保证其质量的稳定性。在具体的修订中，我们主要做了如下三项工作：

1. 根据《职场综合英语教程》(第二版)的内容，把原书中设定为八个单元的练习进行压缩，改成六个单元的练习；

2. 对原书中的部分阅读理解和英译汉内容进行修订，使之与最新英语应用能力考试(B级)接轨；

3. 以新型英语应用能力考试(B级)真题代替业已淘汰的旧真题。

修订后的《职场综合英语实训手册》难度有所降低，更加适合学习者利用课外时间自学，有利于促进学习者对课堂内容的消化，有助于学习者了解和迎接英语应用能力考试。

当然，尽管我们进行了认真的修订，书中仍然可能会存在这样或那样的谬误，希望大家在使用的过程中发现这些不足，及时反馈给我们，以便我们在下次修订时更正。

编者

2017年7月

第一版前言

《职场综合英语教程》是一套由西方文化入手,渐进涉及职场工作需要的高职英语教材。该教材遵循"以服务为宗旨,以就业为导向"的原则,结合高职英语教学的需要和高职学生的实际英语水平,具有较强的实用性和针对性。《职场综合英语实训手册》(第一册)(以下简称《实训手册》),是《职场综合英语教程》(第一册)(以下简称《教程》)的辅助教程,内容与《教程》(第一册)有所兼顾,同时又充分考虑到"高等学校英语应用能力考试(B级)"(以下简称"B级考试")的实考题型,在结构上对"B级考试"的题型进行了套用。这样设计的目的有三:一、增强学生的动手能力,包括记录所听材料的关键词,写摘要,翻译英语语句,用英语写应用文等。二、通过练习检测学生学习《教程》(第一册)的效果,帮助教师了解学生学习中的困难,从而更有效地施教。三、帮助学生了解"B级考试"的要求,以便学生顺利通过这项旨在检测高职学生英语是否合格的等级考试。

《实训手册》(第一册)包含八个单元练习和两套实考题。所有练习均参照"B级考试"的题型和题数,并在内容上尽可能保持与《教程》(第一册)的单元内容一致。在各种题型中,"翻译—英译汉"与"B级考试"中的同类型试题有较大区别,最主要的区别是取消了选择,取消了段落翻译。不过,"翻译—英译汉"所使用的语句全部来自《教程》(第一册)中的课文,从而使《实训手册》(第一册)在内容上与《教程》(第一册)保持了密切的联系。

在对《实训手册》(第一册)进行实际训练时,建议学生把重点放在做题方法上。比如,做"Vocabulary & Structure"的要点是发现题干中的关键词。

例题:

16. The report gives a _____ picture of the company's future development.
  A. central   B. clean   C. clear   D. comfortable

(2010年12月试卷)

做这一题的要点是把题干中的picture看作关键词。所给选项中central表示"中心的";clean表示"清洁的";clear表示"清晰的";comfortable表示"舒服的"。只有clear与picture搭配最好;因此,属于最好选项。

再看一例:

26. Could you tell me the (different) _____ between American and British English in business writing?

(2010年12月试卷)

本题的关键词是空白处前面的tell。所填词显然应该是tell的宾语,different是形容词,不能做宾语,应填differences。

我们再以阅读理解为例。下面是2010年12月"B级考试"的实考题:

MEMO

To： Katherine Anderson, Manager

From： Stephen Black, Sales Department

Date： 19 November, 2010

Subject： Resignation（辞职）

Dear Ms. Katherine Anderson,

  I am writing to inform you of my intention to resign（辞职）from G&S Company.

  I very much appreciate my four years' working for the company. The training has been excellent and I have gained valuable experience working within an efficient and friendly team environment. In particular, I am very grateful for your personal guidance during these first years of my career.

  I feel now that it is time to further develop my knowledge and skills in a different environment.

  I would like to leave, if possible, in a month's time on Saturday, 18 December. This will allow me to complete my current job responsibilities. I hope that this suggested arrangement is acceptable to the company.

  Once again, thank you for your attention.

第一版前言

> **Memo**
>
> Date: 19 November, 2010
> Memo to: Katherine Anderson, (46) _____
> Memo from: (47) _____, Sales Department
> Subject: Resignation
> Years of working for G&S Company: (48) _____
> Reasons for leaving: to further develop (49) _____ in another environment
> Time of leaving the position: on (50) _____

做类似题目的要点是带着题目在原文中找结构,而不是理解原文,因此,很多时候不需要对原文进行逐句阅读。

就上述题目而言,(46)的要点在于填空前面的词:Katherine Anderson;(47)的要点是填空后面的词:Sales Department;(48)的要点在于填空前面的词:G&S Company;(49)的要点在于填空前面的词:further develop;(50)的要点在于填空前面的词:Time 和 on。

根据以上线索不难发现,本题的答案是:(46) Manager;(47) Stephen Black;(48) four/4;(49) knowledge and skills;(50) Saturday, 18 December。

《实训手册》(第一册)由安徽高职外语教研会组织编写,主要编写人员为安徽水利水电职业技术学院的童敬东和袁春梅以及其他学校的骨干教师。在编写过程中我们参考了大量的文字资料,对这些有关资料的编者我们深表感谢。同时,我们也深深知道,尽管我们认真地对本教程进行了审阅,书中错误仍然在所难免。在此,我们诚恳希望各位教师和同学在使用本书的过程中把编写之错漏记下来反馈给我们,以便我们以后通过修订,使本书更臻于完善。

编者

2012 年 6 月

目 录

Unit 1　Success Story ··· (1)
 Part Ⅰ　Listening Comprehension ··· (1)
 Part Ⅱ　Vocabulary & Structure ·· (3)
 Part Ⅲ　Reading Comprehension ·· (5)
 Part Ⅳ　Translation ·· (11)
 Part Ⅴ　Writing ··· (12)

Unit 2　Travelling ··· (13)
 Part Ⅰ　Listening Comprehension ··· (13)
 Part Ⅱ　Vocabulary & Structure ·· (15)
 Part Ⅲ　Reading Comprehension ·· (17)
 Part Ⅳ　Translation ·· (23)
 Part Ⅴ　Writing ··· (24)

Unit 3　English Language ·· (25)
 Part Ⅰ　Listening Comprehension ··· (25)
 Part Ⅱ　Vocabulary & Structure ·· (27)
 Part Ⅲ　Reading Comprehension ·· (29)
 Part Ⅳ　Translation ·· (34)
 Part Ⅴ　Writing ··· (35)

Unit 4　Online Shopping ·· (37)
 Part Ⅰ　Listening Comprehension ··· (37)
 Part Ⅱ　Vocabulary & Structure ·· (39)

Part Ⅲ	Reading Comprehension	(41)
Part Ⅳ	Translation	(47)
Part Ⅴ	Writing	(48)

Unit 5   Advertisement　(50)

Part Ⅰ	Listening Comprehension	(50)
Part Ⅱ	Vocabulary & Structure	(52)
Part Ⅲ	Reading Comprehension	(54)
Part Ⅳ	Translation	(60)
Part Ⅴ	Writing	(61)

Unit 6   Theme Parks　(62)

Part Ⅰ	Listening Comprehension	(62)
Part Ⅱ	Vocabulary & Structure	(64)
Part Ⅲ	Reading Comprehension	(66)
Part Ⅳ	Translation	(72)
Part Ⅴ	Writing	(73)

2017年6月高等学校英语应用能力考试(B级)　(75)

Part Ⅰ	Listening Comprehension	(75)
Part Ⅱ	Vocabulary & Structure	(78)
Part Ⅲ	Reading Comprehension	(80)
Part Ⅳ	Translation — English into Chinese	(86)
Part Ⅴ	Writing	(87)

答案及听力材料 (89)

Unit 1 Success Story

Part I Listening Comprehension

Directions: *This part consists of 3 sections.*

Section A

Directions: *There are 5 recorded questions in it. After each question, there is a pause. The questions will be spoken two times. When you hear a question, you should decide on the correct answer from the 4 choices marked A, B, C and D. Then you should mark your choice.*

1. A. Yes, thank you.
   B. Sorry. I don't know him.
   C. I'm Peter James.
   D. Just fine, thank you. And how are you?

2. A. That's all right.
   B. Ok! Let me introduce you to her.
   C. No, I don't think so.
   D. Sorry. It's too late now.

3. A. You mean James Cameron? No problem.
   B. Sorry. My name is Helen Clinton.

C. He's teaching here for thirty years.

D. Nice to meet you here.

4. A. Take your time. There is no hurry.

B. Thank you very much.

C. Nice to meet you. I'm Michael from IMF.

D. It's not far from here.

5. A. I'm very sorry for what I said.

B. It's five mile from here.

C. I'm afraid I really have to go.

D. I'm going to learn driving. How about you?

Section B

Directions: There are 5 recorded dialogues in it. After each dialogue, there is a recorded question. The dialogues and questions will be spoken only once. When you hear a question, you should decide on the correct answer from the 4 choices marked A, B, C and D. Then you should mark your choice.

6. A. It has stopped raining.　　B. It is still snowing.

   C. It is still raining.　　D. It has cleared up.

7. A. Get a typewriter.　　B. Go out for exercise.

   C. Do some typing.　　D. Buy some paper.

8. A. He never smokes.　　B. He is starting to smoke.

   C. He smoked before now.　　D. He likes smoking.

9. A. The man has been to Canada before.

   B. The man hasn't made up his mind yet.

   C. The man doesn't know where to go.

   D. The man wants to visit Canada.

10. A. She thought she had passed.

    B. She thought it was hard to tell.

    C. It was a failure.

    D. It was interesting.

Unit 1 Success Story

Section C

Directions*: In this section you will hear a recorded short passage. The passage will be read three times. During the second reading, you are required to fill in the missing words or phrases according to what you hear. The third reading is for you to check your writing. Now the passage will begin.*

When a person wants to know someone, he often does so through others' introduction, but in some circumstances, there are no (11)_____, and then self-introduction, which can be very simple, becomes (12)_____. You only have to walk up to the one you want to meet, say "Hello!" to him (13)_____, tell him your name and introduce yourself briefly. Then the one you are speaking to will (14)_____ react to your introduction in a polite way. Of course, there are formal and informal forms of self-introduction. Which one shall we choose? (15)_____. If the two have different social status (社会地位), the formal form should be used.

Part Ⅱ   Vocabulary & Structure

Directions*: This part consists of 2 sections.*

Section A

Directions*: There are 10 incomplete statements here. You are required to complete each statement by choosing the appropriate answer from the 4 choices marked A, B, C, and D.*

16. I didn't answer the phone _____ I didn't hear it ring.
    A. if   B. unless   C. although   D. because

17. Doctor Smith has two sons and one daughter, _____ are all doctors.
    A. who   B. whom   C. that   D. which

18. _____ we think of our happy life today, the more we love our motherland.
    A. How much   B. The more   C. For how much   D. Whatever

19. I don't think _____ worthwhile to take so much trouble to do the job.

    A. this   B. that   C. it   D. those

20. His grandfather is looking forward to _____ to his native place some day.

    A. return   B. being returned   C. be returning   D. returning

21. The young man _____ in this company since he graduated from Madison College five years ago.

    A. works   B. worked   C. was working   D. has been working

22. _____ a wonderful trip he had when he traveled in China!

    A. Where   B. How   C. What   D. That

23. This is a point often overlooked by teachers of language, _____ demand faultless accuracy from the beginning.

    A. who   B. which   C. that   D. though

24. Please _____ your report carefully before you hand it in to me.

    A. turn to   B. bring about   C. go over   D. put up

25. Have you read our letter of December 18, in _____ we complained about the quality of your product?

    A. that   B. where   C. that   D. which

Section B

Directions: There are 10 incomplete statements here. You should fill in each blank with the proper form of the word given in the brackets.

26. We are looking forward to (work) _____ with you in the future.

27. I think he needs some (suggest) _____ on which university he should choose.

28. We can arrange for your car to (repair) _____ within a reasonable period of time.

29. The film turned out to be (success) _____ than we had expected.

30. Economic conditions may be responsible for the (create) _____ of social unrest.

31. Could you tell me the (different) _____ between American and British

Unit 1 Success Story

English in business writing?

32. She managed to settle the argument in a (friend) _____ way.

33. The (bear) _____ of the electric guitar changed country and blues in the 1940s.

34. The people there were really friendly and supplied us with a lot of (use) _____ information.

35. My brother is a (medicine) _____ student specializing in surgery.

Part Ⅲ   Reading Comprehension

Task 1

Directions: *After reading the following passage, you will find 5 questions or unfinished statements. For each question or statement there are 4 choices marked A, B, C and D. You should make the correct choice and mark the corresponding letter.*

To many people, the word Hollywood has two meanings. Hollywood is an area in Los Angeles. Hollywood is also the American movie industry.

Hollywood was just farmland at the beginning of the twentieth century. Early American movies were made in other places, for example, in New York and Chicago.

In 1917 a director was making a movie in Chicago. Because of cold weather, he couldn't finish the movie. He took a trip to southern California, and there he found just the weather and scenery (风景) he needed to finish his movie. The director realized that southern California was the perfect place for making movies. The next year his company built a movie studio in Hollywood. Other companies followed. Before long nearly all important American movie studios were in Hollywood, Los Angeles.

The next thirty years were Hollywood's greatest years. Thousands of movies were made, most by a few large and powerful studios. Directors, actors, and writers worked for these studios. They made some movies that today are considered great art.

Today, Hollywood is not what it was. More movies are made outside of Hollywood. Many studios have moved. The movie stars have also moved to area like Beverly Hills and Malibu.

But visitors to Hollywood today can go to the famous Chinese Theater and see the footprints and autographs (亲笔签名) of movie stars. They can go down the Walk of Fame, on Hollywood Boulevard, and see the golden stars in the sidewalk.

36. Hollywood today means _____.

    A. the movie business and farmland

    B. farmland and perfect scenery

    C. an area in Los Angeles and the movie business

    D. movie stars and their autographs

37. The first American movie studios were built _____.

    A. in Hollywood in 1918   B. in New York and Chicago

    C. in Los Angeles after 1918   D. on California farmland

38. Some movies made in the 1920s to 1940s are considered _____.

    A. golden stars in the sidewalk   B. large and powerful

    C. great art in movie industry   D. famous and glamorous

39. Today, most movies are made _____.

    A. in Beverly Hill   B. outside Hollywood

    C. on Malibu Shore   D. in Hollywood

40. Visitors are still eager to see _____ in Hollywood.

    A. large and powerful studios

    B. the weather and scenery

    C. early American movies produced

    D. footprints and autographs of movie stars

Task 2

Directions: *After reading the following passage, you will find 5 questions or unfinished statements. For each question or statement there are 4 choices marked A, B, C and D. You should make the correct choice and mark the corresponding letter.*

Grandma Moses is among the most celebrated twentieth century painters of the

Unit 1　Success Story

United States, yet she had barely started painting before she was in her late seventies. As she once said of herself, "I would never sit back in rocking chair, waiting for someone to help me." No one could have had a more productive old age.

　　She was born into Anna Mary Robertson on a farm in New York State, one of five boys and five girls. At twelve she left home and was in domestic (家务的；国内的) service until, at twenty-seven, she married Thomas Moses, the hired hand of one of her employers. They farmed most of their lives, first in Virginia and then in New York State, at Eagle Bridge. She had ten children, of whom five survived; her husband died in 1927.

　　Grandma Moses painted a little as a child and made embroidery (刺绣) pictures as a hobby, but only switched to oils in old age because her hands had become too stiff (不易弯曲的) to sew and she wanted to keep busy and pass the time. Her pictures were first sold at the local drugstore and at a fair, and were soon *spotted* by a dealer who bought everything she painted. Three of the pictures were exhibited in the Museum of Modern Art, and in 1940 she had her first exhibition in New York. Between 1930s and her death she painted 2,000 pictures: detailed and lively portrayals of the rural (乡村的) life she had known for so long, with a marvelous sense of color and form. "I think real hard till I think of something real pretty, and then I paint it." she said.

41. Which of the following would be the best title for the passage?
    A. Grandma Moses: A Brief Biography (传记).
    B. Grandma Moses: Her Best Exhibition.
    C. Grandma Moses and other older Artists.
    D. The children of Grandma Moses.

42. According to the passage, Grandma Moses began to paint because she wanted to _____.
    A. keep active   B. decorate (装饰) her house
    C. earn money   D. be a famous artist

43. It can be inferred from the passage that _____.
    A. most of her paintings are about rural life
    B. Grandma Moses knew nothing about painting before she was seventy

C. her husband's death had so great impact on her that she turned to painting for relief

D. her pictures were attractive once appearing in the market

44. Grandma Moses spent most of her life _____.

   A. nursing   B. painting

   C. exhibiting   D. farming

45. The word "spotted" in paragraph 3 could best be replaced by _____.

   A. contributed   B. damaged

   C. noticed   D. nominated

Task 3

Directions: *The following is an introduction. After reading it, you should complete the information by filling in the blanks marked 46 through 50. You should write your answers **in no more than 3 words** on the corresponding space.*

Mary Quant was the inventor of the miniskirt.

Mary Quant was born in London, England on February 11th, 1934. From 1950—1953 she attended Goldsmith's College of Art in London.

In 1955 Marry opened Bazaar, a shop on the Kings Road London, with Alexander Green who later became her husband. Here she sold inexpensive, brightly colored clothes which were immediate hits（成功而风行一时的事物）with young girls and boys.

In 1961 Mary Quant showed her first collection and launched her first wholesale company. In 1962 she presented her first collection for the American market.

She soon built up a million pound industry, selling to nearly all the countries in the western world and Japan. In 1966 she received the O. B. E. （不列颠帝国勋章）for her services to the fashion industry, and went to receive this honor from the Queen dressed in a miniskirt.

In 1970 she introduced hot pants, tight short shorts, worn with floor length maxi-coats（加长大衣）and knee high boots. These were an immediate success.

In 1994 she opened Mary Quant, selling beauty products. In 1996 along with many other designers, she joined a product which was sold for charity and raised

Unit 1　Success Story

quite a good amount.

> ### *Mary Quant*
> Mary Quant was the inventor of the miniskirt. She opened (46)_____ on the Kings Road London, selling inexpensive, brightly colored clothes. In 1961 she launched her first (47)_____. She soon built up a million pound industry, selling to many western countries and (48)_____. In 1966 she received the O. B. E. from the Queen because of her services to (49)_____. In early 1990s she opened Mary Quant, selling (50)_____.

Task 4

Directions: *The following is part of an introduction to a book in which the writer lists fifteen benefits for a good reader. After reading it, you are required to find the items equivalent to（相当于……）those given in Chinese in the table below.*

A — To increase my knowledge

B — To increase my reading enjoyment

C — To better understand what I'm reading

D — To get information that I need on the job

E — To be a more valuable employee

F — To get facts that I need in my personal life

G — To check situations more accurately

H — To help prevent errors and misjudgments

I — To increase my reading skills

J — To become a better speaker and communicator

K — To gather needed background information

L — To improve my writing ability

M — To make better decisions

N — To feel better about myself

O — To help me get ahead in my career

Examples：（L）提高写作能力　　　　（G）对形势做出更准确的评价

51.（　）做个更有价值的雇员　　（　）求得职业生涯上的发展
52.（　）增长知识　　　　　　　（　）搜集个人生活所需的信息
53.（　）提高阅读能力　　　　　（　）做出更好的决定
54.（　）增强自我感觉　　　　　（　）更好地理解所读的内容
55.（　）增加阅读乐趣　　　　　（　）获取工作所需的信息

Task 5

Directions：*The following is an advertisement. After reading it, you will find 3 questions or unfinished statements. For each question or statement there are 4 choices marked A, B, C and D. You should make the correct choice and mark the corresponding letter.*

56. Where are the brand new homes located?

　　A. Close to a famous beach.　　　B. In Castlewood Ranch.
　　C. At New Town.　　　　　　　　D. At Margaret Sandel.

Unit 1 Success Story

57. Living in such homes means convenience for children to _____.

    A. go to school   B. go shopping with their parents

    C. learn to swim   D. learn to drive

58. How much does it cost to live here?

    A. The price is changeable every day.

    B. More than $400 each square meter.

    C. It depends on the number of lodgers（房客）.

    D. It is not suggested in this advertisement.

Part IV   Translation

Directions: *There are 5 sentences, numbered 61 through 65. Write your translation in the corresponding space.*

59. People talked about the role passion played throughout his life and what passion means to today's leaders.

60. After this came a string of successful science-fiction action films.

61. What he told his employees sounds as true today as it did then.

62. Your best days are ahead if you remain passionate about your brand and its benefit to the world.

63. It occurred to him that combining science and art was possible, and he wrote a science-fiction movie with two friends.

Part V Writing

Directions: You are required to write an Invitation Letter based on the following information given in Chinese. Please pay attention to the form of your writing.

说明：写一封邀请信

写信日期：2016 年 9 月 20 日

邀请人：合肥远洋电子公司总经理 Mike Kennedy

被邀请人：Miss Alice Washington

内容包括：合肥远洋电子公司为庆祝公司创立十周年，定于 2016 年 9 月 24 日（星期六）晚上 7 点在安徽饭店举行庆祝晚宴。为了感谢 Alice Washington 多年来的支持和合作，特发邀请。要求收信后回复。

Words for Reference

电子公司 Electronics Corporation

周年 anniversary

庆祝晚宴 dinner party

Unit 2　　Travelling

Part Ⅰ　　Listening Comprehension

Directions: *This part consists of 3 sections.*

Section A

Directions: *There are 5 recorded questions in it. After each question, there is a pause. The questions will be spoken two times. When you hear a question, you should decide on the correct answer from the 4 choices marked A, B, C and D. Then you should mark your choice.*

1. A. Never mind.　　　　　　　B. Yes, I am.
   C. No problem.　　　　　　　D. Here it is.
2. A. I like it very much.　　　　B. That's a good idea.
   C. Thank you.　　　　　　　 D. You're welcome.
3. A. Let's go.　　　　　　　　B. Don't mention it.
   C. It's delicious.　　　　　　D. Here you are.
4. A. He's busy.　　　　　　　 B. He's fine.
   C. He's fifty.　　　　　　　　D. He's a doctor.
5. A. That's difficult.　　　　　　B. It's sunny today.
   C. Yes, please.　　　　　　　D. This way, please.

Section B

Directions: *There are 5 recorded dialogues in it. After each dialogue, there is a recorded question. The dialogues and questions will be spoken only once. When you hear a question, you should decide on the correct answer from the 4 choices marked A, B, C and D. Then you should mark your choice.*

6. A. A telephone.   B. A watch.
   C. A T-shirt.   D. An mp4 player.

7. A. Travel to Australia. B. Start a business.
   C. Work part-time.   D. Write a report.

8. A. Prepare a speech.   B. Send an e-mail.
   C. Type a letter.   D. Make a phone call.

9. A. The first floor.   B. The second floor.
   C. The third floor.   D. The fourth floor.

10. A. In a bank.   B. In a bookstore.
    C. At the airport.   D. At a hotel.

Section C

Directions: *In this section you will hear a recorded short passage. The passage will be read three times. During the second reading, you are required to fill in the missing words or phrases according to what you hear. The third reading is for you to check your writing. Now the passage will begin.*

Britain does not grow rice. The summer is not hot enough. The (11)_____ crop in Britain is wheat. Wheat and other crops grow best in the east of Britain. In the west there is a lot of highland and a lot of (12)_____ . Here grass grows well. So, in the west of Britain, most farms are animal farms. They are not crop farms. The British (13)_____ is mild and the grass grows all the year. (14)_____ live out in the fields and on the highlands. The British people eat a lot of meat and they drink a lot of (15)_____ .

Unit 2 Travelling

Part II Vocabulary & Structure

Directions: *This part consists of 2 sections.*

Section A

Directions: *There are 10 incomplete statements here. You are required to complete each statement by choosing the appropriate answer from the 4 choices marked A, B, C, and D.*

16. Most large companies have a public relations department, _____ tells the public about the company's plans and activities.

    A. which   B. that   C. what   D. how

17. I feel it a great honor for me _____ to this party.

    A. to invite   B. invite   C. to be invited   D. having invited

18. According to the timetable, the train for Beijing _____ at 9:10 p.m. from Monday to Friday.

    A. was leaving   B. is leaving   C. leaves   D. has left

19. I think we'd better _____, otherwise we will be late for the class.

    A. to hurry   B. hurrying up   C. hurried   D. hurry up

20. It was because of his good performance at the interview _____ he got the job with the big company.

    A. so   B. what   C. that   D. while

21. _____ his lecture is short, it gives us a clear picture of the new program.

    A. If   B. Because   C. Although   D. When

22. I am sorry, but I have a question to _____ you.

    A. treat   B. influence   C. ask   D. change

23. Only when we hurried to the airport _____ the flight was cancelled.

    A. we found   B. did we find   C. when   D. weather

24. Please give us the reason _____ the goods were delayed.

    A. why   B. which   C. what   D. how

25. He arrived at New York airport one hour before his _____ to Sydney.

    A. airline   B. plane   C. package   D. flight

Section B

Directions: *There are 10 incomplete statements here. You should fill in each blank with the proper form of the word given in the brackets.*

26. He spoke slowly and with great (difficult) _____ .

27. Mr. Wang's sudden (appear) _____ was worrying all the visitors.

28. It's important to realize how (quick) _____ this disease can spread over the globe.

29. When he was a child, Stephen William Hawking was very interested in (nature) _____ sciences.

30. Because light travels (fast) _____ than sound, lightning is seen before thunder (雷) is heard.

31. She described the ancient city in detail because she (live) _____ there for years.

32. It took me several weeks to get used to (drive) _____ on the left side of the road in London.

33. This medicine is highly (effect) _____ in treating skin cancer if it is applied early enough.

34. Radio and telephone are important means of (communicate) _____ .

35. After all, he is a child and is (possible) _____ to grasp what self-discipline means.

Unit 2 Travelling

Part Ⅲ Reading Comprehension

Task 1

Directions: *After reading the following passage, you will find 5 questions or unfinished statements. For each question or statement there are 4 choices marked A, B, C and D. You should make the correct choice and mark the corresponding letter.*

During our more than 60-year history, with our vast knowledge and experience, Trafalgar has created perfectly designed travel experiences and memories.

Exceptional value

Traveling with Trafalgar can save you up to 40% when compared with traveling independently. We can find you the right hotels, restaurants, and our charges include entrance fees, tolls (道路通行费), etc. Because we're the largest touring company with great buying power, we can pass on our savings to you.

Fast-track entrance

Traveling with us means no standing in line (排队) at major sights. Trafalgar takes care of all the little details, which means you are always at the front of the line.

Travel with like-minded friends

Because we truly are global, you will travel with English-speaking people from around the world, and that leads to life-long friendships.

Great savings

We provide many great ways to save money, including Early Payment Discount (折扣), Frequent Traveler Savings and more.

Fast check-in

Once your booking has been made, you are advised to check in online at our website and meet your fellow travelers before you leave.

36. Because of its great buying power, Trafalgar _____.

　　A. can find the cheapest restaurants

　　B. can pass on its savings to tourists

C. takes tourists to anywhere in the world

D. allows tourists to travel independently

37. Traveling with Trafalgar, tourists do not have to _____.

A. bring their passports with them

B. pay for their hotels and meals

C. stand in line at major sights

D. take their luggage with them

38. Traveling with Trafalgar, tourists may _____.

A. meet tour guides from different countries

B. make new friends from around the world

C. win a special prize offered by the company

D. have a good chance to learn foreign languages

39. Which of the following is mentioned as a way to earn a discount?

A. Early payment.   B. Group payment

C. Office booking.   D. Online booking.

40. After having made the booking, tourists are advised to check in _____.

A. at the hotels   B. at the airport

C. by telephone   D. on the website

Task 2

Directions: *After reading the following passage, you will find 5 questions or unfinished statements. For each question or statement there are 4 choices marked A, B, C and D. You should make the correct choice and mark the corresponding letter.*

A few ways Greyhound can make your next trip even easier

Tickets by Mail. Avoid lining up altogether, by purchasing your tickets in advance, and having them delivered right to your mailbox. Just call Greyhound at least ten days before your departure (1-800-231-2222).

Prepaid Tickets. It's easy to purchase a ticket for a friend or family member no matter how far away they may be. Just call or go to your nearest Greyhound terminal (车站) and ask for details on how to buy a prepaid ticket.

Unit 2　Travelling

Ticketing Requirement. Greyhound now requires that all tickets have travel dates fixed at the time of purchase. Children under two years of age travel free with an adult who has a ticket.

If your destination（目的地）is to Canada or Mexico. Passengers traveling to Canada or Mexico must have the proper travel documents. U. S. , Canadian or Mexican citizens should have a birth certificate, passport or naturalization（入籍）paper. If you are not a citizen of the U. S. , Canada or Mexico, a passport is required. In certain cases a visa may be required as well. These documents will be necessary and may be checked at, or before, boarding a bus departing for Canada or Mexico.

41. From the passage, we can learn that "Greyhound" is probably the name of _____.

    A. an airline　　B. a hotel　　C. a website　　D. a bus company

42. Why should people call Greyhound for tickets in advance?

    A. To avoid waiting in lines at the booking office.

    B. To hand in necessary traveling documents.

    C. To get tickets from the nearest terminal.

    D. To fix the traveling destination in time.

43. What can we learn about the Greyhound tickets?

    A. They are not available for traveling outside the U. S.

    B . Travelers should buy their tickets in person.

    C. Babies can not travel free with their parents.

    D. They have the exact travel date on them.

44. When people are traveling to Canada or Mexico, a passport is a must for _____.

    A. American citizens.　　　　B. Japanese citizens.

    C. Mexican citizens.　　　　 D. Canadian citizens.

45. This passage mainly offers information about _____.

    A. how to prepare documents for traveling with Greyhound

    B. how to purchase a Greyhound ticket and travel with it

    C. how to make your trip with Greyhound interesting

    D. how to travel from the U. S. to Canada and Mexico

Task 3

Directions: *The following is a short passage. After reading it, you should complete the information by filling in the blanks marked 46 to 50. You should write your answers **in no more than 3 words** on the corresponding space.*

Thanks for using Metro（地铁）

Clean. Modern. Safe. And easy to use. No wonder Metro is considered the nation's finest transit（公交）system. This guide tells how to use Metro, and the color-coded map on the inside will help you use Metro to get all around the Nation's Capital.

Metro-rail fares

Each passenger needs a fare-card. (Up to two children under 5 may travel free with a paying customer.)

Fares are based on when and how far you ride. Pay regular fares on weekday's 5:30—9:30 a.m. and 3:00—7:00 p.m. Pay reduced fares at all other times.

Large maps in each station show fares and travel times. Please ask the station manager if you have any questions.

Fare-card machines are in every station. Bring small banknotes because there are no change machines in the stations and fare-card machines only provide up to $5 in change (in coins). Some machines accept credit cards（信用卡）.

A Transit System Metro

Features of the system
1) (46)_____
2) modern
3) safe, and
4) (47)_____

Fares for weekends: (48)_____ fares

Place showing fares and travel times: large maps in (49)_____

Change provided by fare-card machines: up to $ (50)_____

Unit 2 Travelling

Task 4

Directions: *The following is a list of terms related with tourism. After reading it, you are required to find the items equivalent to those given in Chinese in the table below.*

A — gardens   B — custom
C — hot springs   D — steep cliffs
E — sunrise   F — historic relic
G — places of historic interest   H — attractive scenery
I — ancient palace   J — unearthed relics
K — guided tour   L — scenic spot
M — tourist resort   N — tourist attraction
O — sightseeing schedule   P — waterfall
Q — landscape

Example: (B) 风俗   (N) 旅游景点

51. (　) 风景区   (　) 古代宫殿
52. (　) 名胜古迹   (　) 日出
53. (　) 园林   (　) 观光计划
54. (　) 风景秀丽   (　) 温泉
55. (　) 配导游的旅游   (　) 出土文物

Task 5

Directions: *The following is an advertisement. After reading it, you will find 3 questions or unfinished statements. For each question or statement there are 4 choices marked A, B, C and D. You should make the correct choice and mark the corresponding letter.*

56. Who is the organizer of this activity?

    A. English Corner.

    B. Student Union.

    C. Students who have problems in learning English.

    D. English majors who want to make friends.

57. The English Corner activities are regularly held in _____.

    A. different classrooms of Grade 2

    B. Yifu Building Class 3 Grade 2

    C. a meeting room in Yifu Building

    D. gymnasium next to Yifu Building

58. Which of the following is NOT the purpose of the English Corner?

    A. To improve the participants' English level.

    B. To communicate and make friends.

    C. To bring up the interest to English.

    D. To welcome the new students.

Part IV　Translation

Directions: *There are 5 sentences, numbered 61 through 65. Write your translation in the corresponding space.*

59. Digital communication also made backpacking much easier than before.

60. Their purposes of travelling include meeting local people, seeing famous sights, and learning about different cultures.

61. As a result, young people, especially backpackers, prefer hostels to hotels.

62. They were afraid that they might not be able to catch up with their classmates after they returned.

63. They feel exhausted from their high school education and want to understand themselves better outside the classroom.

Part V   Writing

Directions: Laurel Lombard is going to visit Malaysia. You are required to fill in the Malaysia Visa Application Form with her personal information given below in Chinese.

说明：Laurel Lombard,生于 1988 年 2 月 12 日,女,未婚,美国籍,住址 No. 12 Skyscraper Street, New York, N. Y. 12311, U. S. A.。现任 Amazing Legend 公司办公室主任,计划去马来西亚旅行,停留 4 天。申请日期 2016 年 9 月 20 日。

Malaysia Visa Application Form

Full name _____

Date of birth _____

Gender _____   Marital status _____

Citizenship _____   Citizenship at birth _____

Permanent address _____

Present address _____

Occupation _____

Reason for visit _____

Proposed duration of stay _____

Signature _____   Date _____

Unit 3　English Language

Part Ⅰ　Listening Comprehension

Directions: *This part consists of 3 sections.*

Section A

Directions: *There are 5 recorded questions in it. After each question, there is a pause. The questions will be spoken two times. When you hear a question, you should decide on the correct answer from the 4 choices marked A, B, C and D. Then you should mark your choice.*

1. A. Yes, I saw it there.　　　　　　B. I've just finished it.
   C. No, I won't eat.　　　　　　　D. Yes, that's right.
2. A. I'm a doctor.　　　　　　　　B. I'm from Los Angeles.
   C. I'm happy to meet you.　　　　D. Hello. My name is David.
3. A. Right in this building.　　　　　B. Can I help you?
   C. I don't care.　　　　　　　　D. I'd rather you didn't.
4. A. That sounds like fun.　　　　　B. I'm afraid it's getting late.
   C. She's still running a temperature.　D. Please try to come.
5. A. Sorry, I can't help you.　　　　　B. Yes, certainly.
   C. Take it easy.　　　　　　　　D. I appreciate the invitation.

Section B

Directions: *There are 5 recorded dialogues in it. After each dialogue, there is a recorded question. The dialogues and questions will be spoken only once. When you hear a question, you should decide on the correct answer from the 4 choices marked A, B, C and D. Then you should mark your choice.*

6. A. They shouldn't make any more pots.
   B. They should prepare some more coffee.
   C. He will buy another brand.
   D. He doesn't know why people like coffee.

7. A. There's something wrong with their bus.
   B. She doesn't want to go back on either one.
   C. The man can take either one.
   D. She doesn't know when they leave.

8. A. The notice appeared in English and French newspaper.
   B. The advertised jobs are in England and France.
   C. She would like to teach the man English and French.
   D. English and French are necessary for the job.

9. A. It is close to the city.
   B. Fog has forced it to close two or three times.
   C. He has been there only two times.
   D. It is frequently closed because of fog.

10. A. Teach half days.   B. Take a longer tour.
    C. Tour the whole country.   D. Rest for the day.

Section C

Directions: *In this section you will hear a recorded short passage. The passage will be read three times. During the second reading, you are required to fill in the missing words or phrases according to what you hear. The third reading is for you to check your writing. Now the passage will begin.*

We cannot feel speed. But our senses let us know that we are (11) _____.

We see things moving past us and feel that we are being shaken. We can feel acceleration, an (12)_____ in speed. But we notice it for only a short time. For instance, we feel it during the take-off run of an airliner. We feel the plane's acceleration because our bodies do not gain speed (13)_____ the plane does. It seems that something is pushing us back against the seat. Actually, our bodies are trying to stay in the same plane while the plane is (14)_____ us forward. Soon the plane reaches a steady speed. Then, because there is no longer (15)_____ in speed, the feeling of forward motion stops.

Part II Vocabulary & Structure

Directions: *This part consists of 2 sections.*

Section A

Directions: *There are 10 incomplete statements here. You are required to complete each statement by choosing the appropriate answer from the 4 choices marked A, B, C, and D.*

16. Last year, the foreign capital attracted to this city was _____ that of 2010.
    A. twice as many as   B. two times more
    C. twice as much as   D. more than twice

17. We are saving money now _____ we can take a trip in the vacation.
    A. in order to   B. so as to   C. now that   D. so that

18. What are the essential differences _____ selling and marketing?
    A. between   B. from   C. among   D. for

19. Jack called the airline to _____ his flight to Beijing this morning.
    A. confuse   B. reform   C. confirm   D. enable

20. To improve their listening _____, they listen to the news on the radio and watch it on television.
    A. comprehension   B. committee   C. company   D. composition

21. Can you tell me where _____ ?

   A. the new railway station will be built

   B. will be the new railway station built

   C. will the new railway station be built

   D. the new railway station will build

22. The number of the students in a foreign language class _____ usually limited to no more than thirty.

   A. have   B. are   C. is   D. will be

23. To work _____ with the machine, you must read the instructions carefully.

   A. firstly   B. naturally   C. efficiently   D. automatically

24. We'll have to continue the discussion tomorrow _____ we can make a final decision today.

   A. unless   B. because   C. when   D. before

25. By the end of this year Mr. Smith _____ in our company for exactly three years.

   A. is working   B. has worked   C. will work   D. will have worked

Section B

Directions: *There are 10 incomplete statements here. You should fill in each blank with the proper form of the word given in the brackets.*

26. A (self) _____ person thinks much of himself and little of others.

27. Fax machines were a wonderful (invent) _____ at the time.

28. Sometimes I know every word in an (express) _____ , but I don't know what it implies.

29. We must come to a (decide) _____ about what to do next by tomorrow.

30. The most likely (explain) _____ is that his flight was delayed.

31. The bank refused to accept my (apply) _____ for the loan because they weren't convinced by my business plan.

32. My father is a sports fan and he enjoys (swim) _____ very much.

33. The fast (develop) _____ of the local economy has caused serious water pollution in this region.

34. Lily was (luck) _____ enough to get the opportunity to work in that world-famous company.

35. The small village has become (wide) _____ known in recent years for its silk exports.

Part III Reading Comprehension

Task 1

Directions: *After reading the following passage, you will find 5 questions or unfinished statements. For each question or statement there are 4 choices marked A, B, C and D. You should make the correct choice and mark the corresponding letter.*

Each time we produce a new English dictionary, our aim is always the same: what can we do to make the dictionary more helpful for students of English? As a result of our research with students and discussions with teachers, we decided to focus on providing more examples for this English dictionary.

Examples help students to remember the word they have looked up in the dictionary because it is easier both to remember and to understand a word within a context (上下文). The examples also show that words are often used in many different contexts. For these reasons, we have included 40 percent more examples in this new book.

We edit all the examples to remove difficult words and to make sure they are easier to understand.

We very much hope this new book will be of use not only to the students of English but also to the teachers.

36. The aim of the author in producing this new dictionary is to _____.

   A. correct mistakes in the old dictionary

   B. make it more helpful for students

   C. increase the number of words

   D. add pictures and photos

37. A word is easier to remember and understand if it is _____.

   A. included in a word list

   B. pronounced correctly

   C. explained in English

   D. used in a context

38. What is special about this new dictionary?

   A. It is small and cheap.

   B. It has a larger vocabulary.

   C. It has 40% more examples.

   D. It is designed for students and teachers.

39. The purpose of removing difficult words in the examples is to _____.

   A. make them easier to understand

   B. provide more useful words

   C. introduce more contexts

   D. include more examples

40. The passage is most probably taken from _____.

   A. a letter to the editor

   B. a comment on a novel

   C. an introduction to a dictionary

   D. a news-report in the newspaper

Task 2

Directions: *After reading the following passage, you will find 5 questions or unfinished statements. For each question or statement there are 4 choices marked A, B, C and D. You should make the correct choice and mark the corresponding letter.*

People in some countries cannot use their native language for Web addresses. Neither can Chinese speakers, who have to rely on pinyin. But last Friday, ICANN, the Web's governing body, approved the use of up to 16 languages for the new system. More will follow in the coming years.

The Internet is about to start using the 16 languages of the world. People will

Unit 3　English Language

soon be able to use addresses in characters (字符) other than those of the Roman alphabet (字母表). The change will also allow the suffix (后缀) to be expressed in 16 other alphabets, including traditional and simplified Chinese characters.

But there are still some problems to work out. Experts have discussed what to do with characters that have several different meanings. This is particularly true of Chinese.

Most experts doubt the change will have a major effect on how the Internet is used. "There will be some competition between companies to obtain popular words for addresses."

41. For Web addresses, Chinese speakers now have to use _____.
    A. signs　　　B. pinyin　　　C. numbers　　　D. characters

42. The approval of the use of 16 languages by ICANN will allow web users to _____.
    A. change their email address
    B. email their messages in characters
    C. have the chance to learn other languages
    D. use addresses in their own language

43. The new system will allow the suffix of a Web address to be expressed by _____.
    A. any native language　　　B. figures and numbers
    C. Chinese characters　　　D. symbols and signs

44. Which of the following is one of the problems in using the new system?
    A. Certain characters have several different meanings.
    B. Chinese is a truly difficult language to learn.
    C. People find it difficult to type their address in characters.
    D. Some experts think it is impossible to use Chinese characters.

45. Many experts do not believe that _____.
    A. there are still some problems to work out
    B. there will be competition to get popular addresses
    C. companies are willing to change their web addresses
    D. the change will affect the use of the Internet greatly

Task 3

Directions: *The following is a job application letter. After reading it, you should complete the information by filling in the blanks marked 46 to 50. You should write your answers **in no more than 3 words** on the corresponding space.*

Dear Ms. Rennick,

Professor Saul Wilder, an adviser to your firm, has informed me that your company is looking for someone with excellent communication skills, organizational experience, and leadership background for a management position. I believe that my enclosed résumé will show that I have the qualifications（资历）and experience you seek. In addition, I'd like to mention how my work experience as a sales manager last summer makes me a particularly strong candidate for the position.

I would be grateful if you can offer me an opportunity for an interview with you. If you are interested, please contact me at （317）555-0118 any time before 11：00 a.m., or feel free to leave a message. I look forward to meeting with you to discuss the ways my skills may best serve your company.

Sincerely yours,
Richard Smith

An Application Letter

Applicant: Richard Smith

Position applied for: a (46) _____ position

Qualifications required for the position:

1. excellent (47) _____

2. organizational experience

3. (48) _____ background

Work experience (last summer): as (49) _____

Contact number: (50) _____

Enclosure: résumé

Unit 3 English Language

Task 4

Directions: *The following is a list of terms used in railroad services. After reading it, you are required to find the items equivalent to those given in Chinese in the table below.*

A — information desk   B — ticket office
C — half fare ticket   D — waiting room
E — excess baggage charge   F — baggage check-in counter
G — security check   H — platform underpass
I — ticket agent   J — departure board
K — railroad track   L — traffic light
M — railroad crossing   N — soft sleeping car
O — hard sleeping car   P — hard seat
Q — baggage-claim area

Examples:（Q）行李认领处　　　　　（E）超重行李费

51. (　) 硬座　　　　　　　　(　) 软卧
52. (　) 开车时间显示牌　　　(　) 信号灯
53. (　) 站台地下通道　　　　(　) 候车室
54. (　) 问询处　　　　　　　(　) 安全检查
55. (　) 半价票　　　　　　　(　) 售票处

Task 5

Directions: *The following is an advertisement. After reading it, you will find 3 questions or unfinished statements. For each question or statement there are 4 choices marked A, B, C and D. You should make the correct choice and mark the corresponding letter.*

56. When can you begin to buy the discount ticket at the PBA?

   A. January 28.   B. March 7.
   C. March 13.   D. March 30.

57. If you buy the 22 Coupon Ride Sheet on March 7, how much can you save?

   A. $3.   B. $4.
   C. $8.   D. $13.

58. If your 67-year grandmother and 9-year cousin go to the fair, how much should they pay for the general admission?

   A. $8.   B. $12.
   C. $16.   D. $24.

Part Ⅳ Translation

Directions: There are 5 sentences, numbered 61 through 65. Write your translation in the corresponding space.

59. Is it true that it means the same thing if you say, 'The house burned down' or 'The house burned up'?

60. You can say it either way and it means the same thing.

61. Printing brought into English the wealth of new thinking.

62. Some words may be thought beautiful and some ugly; some may live and some may die.

63. Even so simple as expression as "back and forth" arouse confusion, because it is illogical.

Part V Writing

Directions: *You are required to write a thank-you letter to a foreign friend. The following information given in Chinese should be used in your writing.*

说明：写一封感谢信

收信人：*Vincent Freund*

写信时间：2016 年 12 月 26 日。

主要内容：和 *Vincent Freund* 一家人共享平安夜，受到了来自 *Vincent Freund* 及其家人的热情款待，现写信表示感谢。

Words for Reference

平安夜　Christmas Eve

款待　hospitality

感激　gratitude

Unit 4　Online Shopping

Part Ⅰ　Listening Comprehension

Directions: *This part consists of 3 sections.*

Section A

Directions: *There are 5 recorded questions in it. After each question, there is a pause. The questions will be spoken two times. When you hear a question, you should decide on the correct answer from the 4 choices marked A, B, C and D. Then you should mark your choice.*

1. A. Just a moment, please.　　B. Fine, thank you.
   C. See you.　　D. Well done.
2. A. Glad to meet you.　　B. Yes, please.
   C. It may not last long.　　D. In twenty minutes.
3. A. Yes, please.　　B. On Monday.
   C. I see.　　D. Good-bye.
4. A. No problem.　　B. Many times.
   C. I don't know.　　D. My pleasure.
5. A. You are welcome.　　B. He's nice.
   C. It's perfect.　　D. It's two o'clock.

Section B

Directions: *There are 5 recorded dialogues in it. After each dialogue, there is a recorded question. The dialogues and questions will be spoken only once. When you hear a question, you should decide on the correct answer from the 4 choices marked A, B, C and D. Then you should mark your choice.*

6. A. He's got a headache.　　B. He can't sleep at night.
　C. He coughs a lot.　　D. He doesn't feel like eating.
7. A. Have some food.　　B. Clean the table.
　C. Make a phone call.　　D. Buy a dictionary.
8. A. The sales manager.　　B. The information officer.
　C. The office secretary.　　D. The chief engineer.
9. A. Teacher and student.　　B. Manager and secretary.
　C. Police officer and driver.　　D. Husband and wife.
10. A. Asking the way.　　B. Buying a ticket.
　C. Checking in at the airport.　　D. Booking a room.

Section C

Directions: *In this section you will hear a recorded short passage. The passage will be read three times. During the second reading, you are required to fill in the missing words or phrases according to what you hear. The third reading is for you to check your writing. Now the passage will begin.*

Ladies and gentlemen,

It's a great pleasure to have you visit us today. I'm very happy to have the opportunity to (11)_____ our company to you.

The company was established in 1950. We mainly manufacture electronic goods and (12)_____ them all over the world. Our sales were about $100 million last year and our business is growing steadily.

We have offices in Asia, (13)_____ and Europe. We have about 1,000 employees who are actively working to serve the needs of our (14)_____ . In order to further develop our overseas market, we need your help to promote(促销) our products.

I (15)_____ doing business with all of you. Thank you.

Part Ⅱ   Vocabulary & Structure

Directions: *This part consists of 2 sections.*

Section A

Directions: *There are 10 incomplete statements here. You are required to complete each statement by choosing the appropriate answer from the 4 choices marked A, B, C, and D.*

16. If you need more information, please contact us _____ telephone or email.

    A. in   B. by   C. on   D. for

17. My advice was that you _____ smoke in the laboratory.

    A. not   B. don't   C. can't   D. won't

18. My brother brought me a few reference books, but _____ of them was of any use for my report.

    A. neither   B. none   C. either   D. all

19. He was speaking so fast _____ we could hardly follow him.

    A. because   B. that   C. what   D. as if

20. How much does it _____ to take the online training course?

    A. cost   B. pay   C. spend   D. give

21. My suggestion is that the work _____ at once.

    A. will start   B. will be started
    C. be started   D. would be started

22. What he told me to do was _____ I should get fully prepared before the interview.

    A. what   B. that   C. which   D. if

23. We haven't enough rooms for everyone, so some of you will have to _____ a room.

  A. share   B. stay   C. spare   D. live

24. Never in my life _____ the impression made on me by my first visit to New York City.

  A. shall I forget   B. I shall forget   C. forget I   D. do I will forget

25. _____ for your laziness, you could have finished the assignment by now.

  A. Had it not been   C. Weren't it

  B. It were not   D. Had not it been

Section B

Directions: There are 10 incomplete statements here. You should fill in each blank with the proper form of the word given in the brackets.

26. I shall be (interest) _____ to know what happens.

27. What a (wonder) _____ party it was! I enjoyed every minute of it.

28. The managers of a large (organize) _____ may have three levels: top, middle and root levels.

29. The manager has promised that she will deal with the matter (immediate) _____.

30. It was only yesterday that the chief engineer (email) _____ us the details about the project.

31. Today email has become an important means of (communicate) _____ in daily life.

32. The (grow) _____ of online shopping is producing a fundamental change in consumer behavior.

33. When you arrive tomorrow, my secretary (meet) _____ you at the airport.

34. Nowadays, electronic (pay) _____ is a more convenient way to pay for purchases than cash and checks.

35. Community (serve) _____ means helping the people around you.

Unit 4 Online Shopping

Part Ⅲ   Reading Comprehension

Task 1

Directions: *After reading the following passage, you will find 5 questions or unfinished statements. For each question or statement there are 4 choices marked A, B, C and D. You should make the correct choice and mark the corresponding letter.*

Shopping for clothes is not the same experience for a man as it is for a woman. A man goes shopping because he needs something. His purpose is clear and decided in advance. He knows what he wants, and his objective is to find it and buy it; the price is in the second place for consideration. All men simply walk into a shop and ask the assistant for what they want. If the shop has it, the salesman quickly produces it, and the man begins to try it at once. For a man, small problems may begin when the shop does not have what he wants, or does not have exactly what he wants. In that case, the salesman will try to sell the customer something else. Very often, he offers the nearest thing which he can produce.

Now how does a woman go about buying clothes? In almost every respect, she does so in the opposite way. Her shopping is not often based on need. She has never fully made up her mind of what she wants, and she is only "having a look round". She will still be satisfied even if she has bought nothing.

36. How does a man go shopping when he wants to buy something?

   A. He will often ask help from the shop assistant.

   B. He will look at it carefully and wait for a while.

   C. He has made a plan before he wants to buy it.

   D. He will discuss it with his wife and then buy it.

37. What is a man's attitude to the price of goods?

   A. He cares much about it.

   B. He pays little attention to it.

   C. He is often not sure of it.

D. He likes to ask his wife's opinion.

38. What does a man do when he can't get exactly what he wants?

   A. He often looks round the shop.

   B. He will ask the shop assistant for advice.

   C. He will decide to buy something instead.

   D. He doesn't buy anything else.

39. What does a woman usually do when she is going to buy something?

   A. She never arranges a plan for what she is going to buy.

   B. She doesn't ask the shop assistant to help her.

   C. She seldom asks about its price.

   D. She will not try it on in the shop.

40. What is this passage mainly about?

   A. Men's way of buying things.

   B. Women's attitude towards shop assistants.

   C. The difference between men and women in buying things.

   D. Men are better in choosing what they will buy.

Task 2

Directions: *After reading the following passage, you will find 5 questions or unfinished statements. For each question or statement there are 4 choices marked A, B, C and D. You should make the correct choice and mark the corresponding letter.*

If you have an *AT&T Business Direct* account, you can have your telephone bill paid automatically each month. You can make payments online with a bank account or use one of the following credit cards (信用卡): *Visa*, *Master Card*, *Discover Network* or *American Express*. When you make an online payment, please follow the instructions given below.

Instructions

1. To make your payment online, click (点击) the "Pay Now" link under the "Account Overview (概览)" summary.

2. If your business has more than one registered account, first select the account you need from the "Account Number" menu, and then click the "Pay Now" link.

3. If you have never made an online payment before, you will be asked whether you want to make a payment by using a bank account or credit card. Select either "Bank Account" or "Credit Card" from the "Select payment Method" menu.

The online payment system is available Monday through Saturday, from 7:00 AM to 12:00 AM (Midnight) Eastern Time.

41. An *AT&T Business Direct* account helps you _____.

   A. earn an interest from the bank account

   B. make the first month's payment only

   C. pay your telephone bill automatically

   D. enjoy all the available banking services

42. The payment with an *AT&T Business Direct* account can be made online with _____.

   A. a passport   B. a credit card

   C. a driving license   D. a traveller's check

43. If you have several registered accounts for payment, the first link that you should click is _____.

   A. "Select Payment Method" menu   B. "Account Overview" summary

   C. the "Account Number" menu   D. the "Pay Now" link

44. When making the first-time online payment, you will be asked to _____.

   A. register your online account number

   B. open several registered accounts

   C. select the payment method first

   D. apply for a new credit card

45. The passage is mainly about _____.

   A. how to pay phone bills by *AT&T Business Direct*

   B. how to open an *AT&T Business Direct* account

   C. how to make use of online bank services

   D. how to start a small online business

Task 3

Directions: *Read the following passage. After reading it, you should complete the information by filling in the blanks marked 46 to 50. You should write your answers **in no more than 3 words** on the corresponding space.*

Tea drinking was common in China for nearly one thousand years before anyone in Europe had ever heard about tea. People in Britain were much slower in finding out what tea was like, mainly because tea was very expensive. It could not be bought in shops and even those who could afford to have it sent from Holland had little knowledge about tea. They thought it was a vegetable and tried cooking the leaves. Then they served them mixed with butter and salt. They soon discovered their mistake but many people used to spread the used tea leaves on bread and give them to their children as sandwiches.

Tea remained scarce and very expensive in England until the ships of the East India Company began to bring it direct from China early in the seventeenth century. During the next few years so much tea came into the country that the price fell and many people could afford to buy it.

At the same time people on the Continent were becoming more and more fond of tea. Until then tea had been drunk without milk in it, but one day a famous French lady named Madame de Sevigne decided to see what tea tasted like when milk was added. She found it so pleasant that she would never again drink it without milk. Because she was such a great lady her friends thought they must copy everything she did, so they also drank their tea with milk in it. Slowly this habit spread until it reached England and today only very few Britons drink tea without milk.

At first, tea was usually drunk after dinner in the evening. No one ever thought of drinking tea in the afternoon until a duchess (公爵夫人) found that a cup of tea and a piece of cake at three or four o'clock stopped her getting "a sinking feeling" as she called it. She invited her friends to have this new meal with her and so, tea-time was born.

Unit 4 Online Shopping

British people had little (46)_____ about tea. They thought it was (47)_____ and they cooked it. They mixed it with butter and salt. They spread the (48)_____ on bread and called them sandwiches.

A famous French lady found that it was pleasant to drink tea with (49)_____ in it. Later this habit spread to England.

(50)_____ was born because of a duchess. She found that a cup of tea and a piece of cake could stop her getting "a sinking feeling" in the afternoon.

Task 4

Directions: *The following is a list of terms related to the shipment of products. After reading it, you are required to find the items equivalent to those given in Chinese in the table below.*

A — Guard against damp
B — Handle with care
C — Keep away from heat
D — Keep away from cold
E — Keep dry
F — Keep flat
G — No naked fire
H — No use of hooks
I — Not to be thrown down
J — Open here
K — Open in dark room
L — Protect against breakage
M — Poison
N — Take care
O — This side up
P — To be kept upright
Q — Use no knives

Examples:（G）严禁明火　　　　　　（H）禁用吊钩

51.（　）远离热源　　　　　（　）请勿用刀
52.（　）此面朝上　　　　　（　）此处开启
53.（　）竖立安放　　　　　（　）暗室开启
54.（　）小心轻放　　　　　（　）注意平放
55.（　）不可抛掷　　　　　（　）保持干燥

Task 5

Directions: *The following is an advertisement. After reading it, you will find 3 questions or unfinished statements. For each question or statement there are 4 choices marked A, B, C and D. You should make the correct choice and mark the corresponding letter.*

If you are available a few hours during the day, some evenings and occasional weekends to care for two school-aged children, please call Gayle Moore days 800-1111, evenings and weekends 800-4964.

WAITRESS WANTED: 10 a.m.—2 p.m. or 10:30 a.m.—5 p.m. Apply in person, 207 S. Mai. Crutis Restaurant.

56. The babysitter's required to take care of _____.

　　A. two small pets

Unit 4 Online Shopping

B. two children

C. Gayle Moore

D. Mai. Crutis Restaurant

57. Those who want to apply for the babysitter should be available _____.

   A. every day from Monday through Friday

   B. every workday

   C. a few hours each day, some evenings and weekends

   D. whenever the employer asks for assistance

58. Those who want to apply for the waitress should _____.

   A. call the manager

   B. send an e-mail

   C. fill in a registration form

   D. go to the restaurant

Part IV   Translation

Directions: *There are 5 sentences, numbered 61 through 65. Write your translation in the corresponding space.*

59. All they have to do are just browse for the product they want in the website and within a few mouse clicks they are off.

60. Even though online merchants have tried their best to improve the security, threats and attacks still prevail.

61. Consumers should limit themselves from releasing unnecessary personal information such as age and income to protect their privacy.

62. You can shop from retailers in other parts of the country or even the world without being limited by geographic area.

63. Because of the numerous advantages and benefits of shopping online more and more people these days prefer online shopping over conventional shopping.

Part Ⅴ Writing

Directions: *You are required to complete an E-mail Message for Room Reservations. Some information and the e-mail form are given to you.*

说明：写一份电子邮件

写信人：Tammy Foxworthy

入住时间：2016 年 12 月 25 日至 27 日

主要内容：预订房间。要求一个带浴室的单人房间，三个带浴室的双人房间。拟于 12 月 26 日下午租用会议室一间，进行业务洽谈。希望对方尽早回复，并告知是否有空房，房价是多少，以及是否需要预付押金等。

Unit 4 Online Shopping

Words for Reference

空房 vacancy； 预付押金 pay a deposit

To：groupsales@aston.com
From：foxworthy@126.com
Subject：
Date：Dec. 20，2016
Dear Sir or Madam，

Unit 5 Advertisement

Part Ⅰ Listening Comprehension

Directions: *This part consists of 3 sections.*

Section A

Directions: *There are 5 recorded questions in it. After each question, there is a pause. The questions will be spoken two times. When you hear a question, you should decide on the correct answer from the 4 choices marked A, B, C and D. Then you should mark your choice.*

1. A. It is you, Eric. What a surprise!
   B. Yes, it's much better than yesterday.
   C. Yeah, I went to Paris for this vocation.
   D. It's on the left corner just ahead.

2. A. Yes, it's one of the most beautiful places I've ever been to.
   B. I'll see you off at the airport.
   C. That's really kind of you.
   D. Maybe you'd better see a doctor.

3. A. Well, take care of yourself.
   B. Nice to meet you. I'm Elvis Presley.

Unit 5 Advertisement

C. Certainly, sir. We'll have to fill out some forms.

D. I do apologize for that.

4. A. So soon? Everybody is having a good time.

B. Yes, I do need your help.

C. No, thanks. I had two cups just now.

D. Just fine, thanks. And how are you?

5. A. Sorry for having caused you a lot of trouble.

B. I hope this will not happen again.

C. I'm afraid I can't do anything.

D. Please let me know whenever you need help.

Section B

Directions: *There are 5 recorded dialogues in it. After each dialogue, there is a recorded question. The dialogues and questions will be spoken only once. When you hear a question, you should decide on the correct answer from the 4 choices marked A, B, C and D. Then you should mark your choice.*

6. A. Go to the concert.   B. Work in the office.
   C. Attend a party.   D. Stay at home.

7. A. Customer and salesman.   B. Patient and doctor.
   C. Teacher and student.   D. Husband and wife.

8. A. She went to see a friend.   B. She had no class.
   C. Her mother took her to hospital. D. Her mother was ill.

9. A. The man will take a flight. B. The man will leave at once.
   C. The flight will leave at 2:30. D. The flight will be late.

10. A. It's on the right of the man. B. It's on Rose Street.
    C. It's far from Rose Street.   D. It's around the next corner.

Section C

Directions: *In this section you will hear a recorded short passage. The passage will be read three times. During the second reading, you are required to fill* *in the missing words or phrases according to what you hear. The third reading is for you to check your writing. Now the passage will begin.*

Ladies and Gentlemen,

Welcome to you all. We are pleased to have you here to visit our company.

Today, we will first (11) _____ you around our company, and then you will go and see our (12) _____ and research center. The research center was built (13) _____ .

You may ask any questions you have during the visit. We will (14) _____ to make your visit comfortable and worthwhile.

Again, I would like to extend a warmest welcome to all of you on behalf of our company, and I hope that you will enjoy your stay here and (15) _____ .

Part Ⅱ Vocabulary & Structure

Directions: *This part consists of 2 sections.*

Section A

Directions: *There are 10 incomplete statements here. You are required to complete each statement by choosing the appropriate answer from the 4 choices marked A, B, C, and D.*

16. Paul doesn't have to be made _____ . He always works hard.

    A. learn   B. to learn   C. to learning   D. learning

17. Another example is that Americans do not eat dogs, _____ people from some other cultures regard them as good food.

    A. though   B. therefore   C. when   D. because

18. We see _____ other people in our culture do things, and we do them in the same way.

    A. what   B. why   C. how   D. where

19. She's very clever, very beautiful, and _____ , very popular.

    A. above all   B. after all   C. in all   D. all in all

Unit 5　Advertisement

20. We are happy at the good news _____ Mr. Black has been awarded the Best Manager.

    A. that　　　B. which　　　C. what　　　D. when

21. It is important that we _____ the task ahead of time.

    A. will finish　　　　　　　B. finished

    C. finish　　　　　　　　　D. having finished

22. _____ in the company for five years, Ray Mahoney has become experienced in business negotiations.

    A. Having worked　　　　　B. Have been worked

    C. Have worked　　　　　　D. Worked

23. _____ their differences, they fell passionately in love with each other.

    A. As for　　　B. Owing to　　　C. Despite　　　D. Through

24. There were two small rooms in the beach house, _____ served as a kitchen.

    A. the smaller of which　　　B. the smaller of them

    C. the smallest of which　　　D. smallest of the two

25. Breakfast can be _____ to you in your room for an additional charge.

    A. eaten　　　B. served　　　C. used　　　D. made

Section B

Directions: *There are 10 incomplete statements here. You should fill in each blank with the proper form of the word given in the brackets.*

26. Teenagers went crazy over his amazing voice and his (attract) _____ performances.

27. After making an appointment, generally, don't change it as that is (polite) _____.

28. If your neighbors are too noisy, then you have a good reason to make your (complain) _____.

29. The visitors were (disappoint) _____ to find the museum closed when they rushed there.

30. The lecturer tried to make his speech (excite) _____ so that the

audience would not feel sleepy.

31. His (care) _____ caused his failure in the final examination eventually.

32. Measures should be taken to avoid the negative effect (bring) _____ about by unfair competition.

33. Did you have any trouble (drive) _____ through the snow?

34. The government is trying to find a way to deal with the problem of pollution (effective) _____.

35. Look at the terrible situation I am in now! If only I (follow) _____ your suggestion.

Part Ⅲ Reading Comprehension

Task 1

Directions: *After reading the following passage, you will find 5 questions or unfinished statements. For each question or statement there are 4 choices marked A, B, C and D. You should make the correct choice and mark the corresponding letter.*

Online advertising is the means of selling a product on the Internet. With the arrival of the Internet, the business world has become digitalized (数字化) and people prefer buying things online, which is easier and faster. Online advertising is also known as e-advertising. It offers a great variety of services, which can not be offered by any other way of advertising.

One major benefit of online advertising is the immediate spread of information that is not limited by geography or time. Online advertising can be viewed day and night throughout the world. Besides, it reduces the cost and increases the profit of the company.

Small businesses especially find online advertising cheap and effective. They can focus on their ideal customers and pay very little for the advertisements.

In a word, online advertising is a cheap and effective way of advertising, whose success has so far fully proved its great potential (潜力).

Unit 5 Advertisement

36. According to the first paragraph, buying things online is more _____.
    A. convenient B. traditional
    C. reliable D. fashionable

37. Compared with any other way of advertising, online advertising _____.
    A. attracts more customers
    B. displays more samples
    C. offers more services
    D. makes more profits

38. Which of the following statements is TRUE of online advertising?
    A. It has taken the place of traditional advertising.
    B. It will make the Internet technology more efficient.
    C. It can help sell the latest models of digitalized products.
    D. It can spread information without being limited by time.

39. Who can especially benefit from online advertising?
    A. Local companies.
    B. Small businesses.
    C. Government departments.
    D. International organizations.

40. This passage is mainly about _____.
    A. the function and the use of the Internet
    B. the application of digital technology
    C. the development of small businesses
    D. the advantages of online advertising

Task 2

Directions: *After reading the following passage, you will find 5 questions or unfinished statements. For each question or statement there are 4 choices marked A, B, C and D. You should make the correct choice and mark the corresponding letter.*

Pressure Cooker (压力锅) Safety

When you are cooking with a pressure cooker, you should learn a few common sense rules.

1. Never leave the cooker unwatched when it is in use.

2. Add sufficient liquid but never past the recommended fill point. Overfilling the cooker may block the vent pipe and cause the cooker to explode.

3. Set the cooker time. Too much time may overcook the food or too much pressure may build up in the cooker. Too little time will lead to undercooked food.

4. If you are new to pressure cooking, follow the cooking instructions carefully. Heat and time can either result in a great meal or a ruined one.

5. Never try to force a pressure cooker cover open. Allow the cooker to cool or run it under cool water before trying to open the cover.

6. Clean the cooker after each use. Mild detergent(洗洁剂) and hot water work the best. Do not use stove ash or sand for they may damage the cooker. The gasket (垫圈) is best cleaned in warm soapy water and then dried. Store the gasket in the bottom of the pot.

41. According to the first rule, the user should _____.

    A. keep the cooker under close watch

    B. always keep the cooker half full

    C. never leave the cooker empty

    D. never turn off the stove

42. According to the second rule, too much liquid in the cooker may result in _____.

    A. a ruined meal   B. undercooked food

    C. too little pressure   D. a blocked vent pipe

43. According to the fifth rule, a pressure cooker cover should be opened _____.

    A. as soon as the cooking is finished

    B. while it is still on the stove

    C. with force when it is hot

    D. after it is cooled down

44. According to the instructions, which of the following is true?

    A. The gasket should be cleaned with cold water.

B. Mild detergent and hot water can best clean the cooker.

C. Soapy water will often damage the cooker.

D. Sand can be used to clean the cooker.

45. Which of the following operations may be dangerous?

A. Overfilling the cooker with food and water.

B. Cleaning the cooker with detergent.

C. Cooling the cooker with cold water.

D. Setting too little cooking time.

Task 3

***Directions**: The following is a letter of complaint. After reading it, you should complete the information by filling in the blanks marked 46 to 50. You should write your answers **in no more than 3 words** on the corresponding space.*

December 10th, 2016

Dear Sirs,

I'm writing to tell you that your latest shipment (装运) of apples is not up to the standard we expected from you. Many of them are bruised (擦伤), and more than half are covered with little spots. They are classed as Grade A, but I think there must have been some mistake, as they are definitely not Grade A apples.

We have always been satisfied with the quality of your produce (农产品), which makes this case all the more puzzling. I would be grateful if you could look into the matter. We would be happy to keep the apples and try to sell them at a reduced price, but in that case we would obviously need a credit (部分退款) from you. Alternatively, you could collect them and replace them with apples of the right quality. Would you please phone me to let me know how you want to handle it?

Yours faithfully,

Fiona Stockton

Purchasing Manager

A Letter of Complaint

Produce involved: Grade A (46)_____.

Causes of complaint:

   1. many of the apples are bruised

   2. more than half of the apples are covered with (47)_____.

Suggested solutions:

   1. allow to sell at (48)_____ and give (49)_____, or

   2. collect them and replace them with apples of (50)_____.

Task 4

Directions: *The following is a list of different types of advertising. After reading it, you are required to find the items equivalent to those given in Chinese in the table below.*

   A — action advertising   B — airport advertising

   C — billboard advertising   D — business advertising

   E — direct mail advertising   F — gift advertising

   G — lamp post advertising   H — light box advertising

   I — local advertising   J — magazine advertising

   K — neon light advertising   L — newspaper advertising

   M — online advertising   N — outdoor advertising

   O — platform side advertising   P — public service advertising

   Q — sales promotion advertising

Examples: (P) 公益广告   (K) 霓虹灯广告

51. ( ) 机场广告		( ) 户外广告
52. ( ) 灯箱广告		( ) 杂志广告
53. ( ) 地方性广告		( ) 路灯柱广告
54. ( ) 赠品广告		( ) 直接邮递广告
55. ( ) 行为广告		( ) 报纸广告

Unit 5 Advertisement

Task 5

Directions: *The following is an advertisement. After reading it, you will find 3 questions or unfinished statements. For each question or statement there are 4 choices marked A, B, C and D. You should make the correct choice and mark the corresponding letter.*

TREAT YOURSELF TO HOME ENERGY SAVINGS.

It's the best time to save with this great offer from New Jersey's Clean Energy Program. Take the Change A Light Pledge to change at least one light bulb in your home to an energy-efficient bulb.

It's the bright thing to do, since ENERGY STAR qualified compact fluorescent light (CFL) bulbs:
- Last 6 to 10 times longer than standard bulbs
- Use two-thirds less energy
- Save you at least $30 in energy costs over the life of a single bulb

By changing one light—and helping us reach our goal of at least 15,000 pledges—you can help reduce energy usage and lower greenhouse gas emissions. It's one of many ways you can help us all achieve Governor Corzine's energy vision for the future.

SAVE 75% NOW on ENERGY STAR® qualified bulbs at a retailer near you.

Learn more about ENERGY STAR and take the Change A Light Pledge today at:
NJCleanEnergy.com

New Jersey's Clean Energy Program
Your Power to Save
njcleanenergy.com
New Jersey Board of Public Utilities
Office of Clean Energy

CHANGE A LIGHT CHANGE THE WORLD
ENERGY STAR

56. Compared with standard bulbs, energy-efficient bulb can last _____.

   A. more than 15,000 days

   B. 6 to 10 times shorter

   C. about 30 times longer

   D. 6 to 10 times longer

57. How much money can we save if we use energy-efficient bulb?

   A. More than $30 over a single bulb.

   B. About $6 or $10 over a single bulb.

   C. Less than $30 a year.

   D. About $6 or $10 each night.

58. What is the benefit of using energy-efficient bulb?

A. People will learn more about greenhouse gas emissions.

B. Energy usage will not be as much as before.

C. 75% energy costs will be saved.

D. People will know how to save energy.

Part IV Translation

Directions: *There are 5 sentences, numbered 61 through 65. Write your translation in the corresponding space.*

59. They simply share their experience and their opinion with their friends and family.

60. Customers who have problems that are satisfactorily resolved are far more likely to be loyal, and to say good things about your company.

61. Complaints are a great way to learn about what your customers are thinking and feeling.

62. Creating an advertisement for a product or a service seems to be a difficult task for many.

63. Make a list of your product benefits and then rank them in the order of importance to your consumer.

Unit 5 Advertisement

Part Ⅴ Writing

Directions: *You are required to write an application letter according to the information given in Chinese. Please pay attention to the form of your writing.*

说明：写一封求职信

写信人：荣芝。

手机号码：15876345235

内容包括：在 2016 年 11 月 13 日的《新安晚报》上看到贵公司招聘英语导游的广告。本人 2013 年 9 月至 2016 年 6 月在淮南职业技术学院学习旅游专业。上学期间利用业余时间做过导游，自信能胜任工作。

Unit 6　Theme Parks

Part Ⅰ　Listening Comprehension

Directions: This part consists of 3 sections.

Section A

Directions: There are 5 recorded questions in it. After each question, there is a pause. The questions will be spoken two times. When you hear a question, you should decide on the correct answer from the 4 choices marked A, B, C and D. Then you should mark your choice.

1. A. No problem.　　　　　　　B. A good idea.
   C. My pleasure.　　　　　　　D. Of course not.
2. A. After December 24.　　　　B. In East Europe.
   C. In the countryside.　　　　D. It's too hot in June.
3. A. It was impossible.　　　　B. So do I.
   C. It was wonderful.　　　　　D. I see.
4. A. You are welcome.　　　　　B. Long time no see.
   C. How are you?　　　　　　　D. Sure. Where?
5. A. I'm not sure.　　　　　　　B. Glad to meet you.
   C. Go ahead.　　　　　　　　　D. No, thanks.

Unit 6 Theme Parks

Section B

Directions: *There are 5 recorded dialogues in it. After each dialogue, there is a recorded question. The dialogues and questions will be spoken only once. When you hear a question, you should decide on the correct answer from the 4 choices marked A, B, C and D. Then you should mark your choice.*

6. A. Water. B. Coffee.
   C. Tea. D. Beer.
7. A. The line is busy. B. There is no taxi.
   C. The traffic is heavy. D. He can't call a taxi for her.
8. A. Husband and wife. B. Teacher and student.
   C. Patient and doctor. D. Manager and secretary
9. A. By bus. B. On foot.
   C. By car. D. By bike.
10. A. Buy a new computer. B. Try the computer again.
    C. Have the computer repaired. D. Use her computer.

Section C

Directions: *In this section you will hear a recorded short passage. The passage will be read three times. During the second reading, you are required to fill in the missing words or phrases according to what you hear. The third reading is for you to check your writing. Now the passage will begin.*

Today more and more people begin to understand that study does not come to an end with school graduation. Education is not just a college (11)_____; it is life itself. Many people are not interested in studying at a college, and they are interested in (12)_____ of learning. They may go to a (13)_____ in their own field; they may improve their (14)_____ skills by following television courses. They certainly know that if they know more or learn more, they can get (15)_____ jobs or earn more money.

Part II　Vocabulary & Structure

Directions: *This part consists of 2 sections.*

Section A

Directions: *There are 10 incomplete statements here. You are required to complete each statement by choosing the appropriate answer from the 4 choices marked A, B, C, and D.*

16. The car industry can't survive _____ the government help.

    A. without   B. with   C. besides   D. except

17. Such problems _____ air and water pollutions have to be solved as soon as possible.

    A. like   B. as   C. of   D. about

18. The first record was not satisfactory, _____.

    A. so was the second   B. the second was too

    C. neither was the second   D. the second was neither

19. I had considerable difficulty _____ her to go out for a drink with me.

    A. to persuade   B. to have persuaded

    C. persuade   D. persuading

20. Many students didn't know the answer _____ the teacher had told them again and again.

    A. even   B. in spite of   C. while   D. although

21. _____ long trousers, long-sleeved shirt fastened at the end is also necessary.

    A. Except   B. Beside

    C. In addition   D. In addition to

22. However, _____ his great wealth, Nobel was not a happy man.

    A. despite of   B. nevertheless

    C. in spite of   D. unless

Unit 6 Theme Parks

23. The next board meeting will focus _____ the benefits for the employees.
    A. by   B. for   C. with   D. on

24. It is required that such insulator (绝热体) _____ a heat-resistant material.
    A. make   B. to be make from
    C. be made of   D. making

25. Many companies provide their employees _____ free lunch during the weekdays.
    A. by   B. with   C. to   D. for

Section B

Directions: *There are 10 incomplete statements here. You should fill in each blank with the proper form of the word given in brackets.*

26. Thomas was cheerful and (help) _____, and we soon became good friends.

27. The more careful you are, the (well) _____ you will be able to complete the work.

28. A (combine) _____ of several mistakes led to the terrible traffic accidents.

29. The past decade has seen great economic (develop) _____ in this country.

30. If the engineer (come) _____ here yesterday, the problem would have been solved.

31. John is the (good) _____ engineer we have ever hired in our department.

32. Now many young people spend several hours a day (talk) _____ on a mobile phone.

33. In China, it is quite (nature) _____ for people to go back home for the Spring Festival.

34. We have so many people walking around who are (die) _____ and they don't even know it!

35. Advances in medical technology have made it possible for people (live) _____ longer.

Part Ⅲ　Reading Comprehension

Task 1

Directions：*After reading the following passage, you will find 5 questions or unfinished statements. For each question or statement there are 4 choices marked A, B, C and D. You should make the correct choice and mark the corresponding letter.*

Fossils（化石）tell us that animals, such as fishes, reptiles（爬行动物）and large mammals（哺乳动物）, lived on earth many millions of years before man. Later, early man's life was always threatened by the huge animals which wandered the world. Today, the situation is reversed（相反）. Many wild animals are threatened by man. In the press, attention is most often concentrated on the problems of the whale, but many other animals are in danger, too. Here is a case in point—the American bison（野牛）.

In the year 1700, about 60 million bison wandered freely in North America. Their range was very wide and they were still growing in numbers despite being hunted by Indians. Today, the bison population of North America is around 10 000, a mere fraction of the former total. How was this terrible decrease come about? The white man and his rifle must take the blame. During the building of the Union Pacific Railway, the bison was hunted more for pleasure than for its meat. By the 1890s, only a few hundred bison were left. The recent increase in numbers has been made possible only by strict government control over hunting. Now the bison is threatened more by disease than by hunters. Its breeding areas are all protected.

36. According to the article, the earlier forms of life on earth were _____.
　　A. whales　　　B. animals　　C. bison　　　D. man
37. The decrease of American bison number during the past few centuries is mainly due to _____.

A. the building of the Union Pacific Railway

B. being hunted by Indians

C. being hunted by white people

D. various kinds of diseases

38. It seems that although they were being hunted by Indians before the eighteenth century, _____.

   A. the bison population was still increasing

   B. the bison population was decreasing sharply

   C. they could still live on peacefully

   D. there were few areas where they could wander freely

39. Now the worst enemy of the bison is _____.

   A. strict government control   B. disease

   C. man   D. hunters

40. What is implied but not stated in the article is that _____.

   A. the hunting of the bison is now under strict government control

   B. by the 1890s the bison population had been reduced to a few hundred

   C. newspapers pay much attention to the problems of the whale

   D. the bison meat is eatable

Task 2

Directions: *After reading the following passage, you will find 5 questions or unfinished statements. For each question or statement there are 4 choices marked A, B, C and D. You should make the correct choice and mark the corresponding letter.*

There is no denying it: Boys think differently from girls. Even though recent brain research evidence is controversial, that conclusion seems inescapable (不可忽视的). One clue to brain differences between the sexes came from observation of infants. One study found that from shortly after birth, females are more sensitive to certain types of sounds, particularly to a mother's voice. Female babies are also more easily startled by loud noises.

Tests show that girls have increased skin sensitivity, particularly in the fingertips, and are better at fine motor performance. Female infants speak sooner, have large vocabularies and rarely demonstrate speech defects (缺陷). (Stuttering, for instance, occurs almost exclusively (独有的) among boys.) Girls exceed boys in language abilities, and this early linguistic bias (特殊能力) often prevails throughout life. Girls read sooner, learn foreign languages more easily and as a result, are more likely to enter occupations involving language mastery.

Boys, in contrast, show an early visual superiority. They are also clumsier, performing poorly at something like arranging a row of bead, but excel at other activities calling on total body coordination (协调). A study of preschool children by psychologist Diane McGuinness of Stanford University found boys more curious, especially in regard to exploring their environment. Her studies also confirmed that males are better at manipulating three-dimensional space.

There is evidence that some of these differences in performance are differences in brain organization between boys and girls. Overall, verbal (语言的) and spatial (空间的) abilities in boys tend to be "packaged" into different hemispheres: the right hemisphere for nonverbal tasks, the left for verbal tasks. But in girls nonverbal skills are likely to be found on both sides of the brain. The hemispheres of women's brains may be less specialized for these functions.

These differences are believed by some scientists to provide a partial explanation of why members of one sex or the other are underrepresented in certain professions. Architects, for example, require a highly developed spatial sense, a skill found more frequently among men.

41. The topic of this passage is on _____.

    A. boys' superiority over girls

    B. girls' superiority over boys

    C. the brain differences between boys and girls

    D the different requirements of boys and girls

42. According to the passage, which of the following statements is true?

    A. Females have a better spatial sense.

    B. Female babies are more sensitive to a mother's voice.

    C. Boys exceed girls in audio abilities.

Unit 6　Theme Parks

D. Girls exceed boys in visual abilities.

43. Boys are usually good at _____.

    A. arranging a row of beads

    B. fine motor performance

    C. manipulating three-dimensional space

    D. stuttering

44. Nonverbal skills in girls' brains can probably be found _____.

    A. in the right hemisphere

    B. in the left hemisphere

    C. both A and B

    D. none of the above

45. Females are underrepresented in the profession of architecture because _____.

    A. they are not so curious as males

    B. they cannot call on total body coordination

    C. they are treated with prejudice

    D. their spatial sense is not so highly developed as males

Task 3

Directions: *Read the following passage. After reading it, you should complete the information by filling in the blanks marked 46 to 50. You should write your answers **in no more than 3 words** on the corresponding space.*

Make our Tourist Information Centre your first call when planning your visit to Cheltenham. Our friendly team can provide a wide range of services to make your stay enjoyable and unforgettable. We can book your accommodation (住宿), from a homely bed and breakfast to a four-star hotel. We can provide tickets for local events and we are booking agents (代理商) for National Express and other local coach companies.

In summer we organize our own various programs of Coach Tours of the Cotswolds, plus regular walking tours around Cheltenham, all guided by qualified guides. We also stock a wide range of maps and guidebooks plus quality gifts and souvenirs(纪念品). We can help you with advice on what to see, where to go and how to get there.

We look forward to seeing you in Cheltenham.

Tours of Cheltenham

Tour Services Provider: (46)_____

Services Offered:

1. booking accommodation
2. providing tickets for (47)_____
3. booking tickets from National Express and other (48)_____
4. organizing Coach Tours and regular (49)_____ in summer
5. providing various maps, (50)_____, gifts and souvenirs

Task 4

Directions: The following is a list of terms used as signs. After reading it, you are required to find the items equivalent to those given in Chinese in the table below.

A — Admission free   B — Keep away from fire
C — No Admittance   D — No Entry
E — Drive slowly   F — No Peeling
G — No Scribbling   H — No Spitting
I — Paste no bills   J — Visiting Hours
K — Keep off the grass   L — Don't touch
M — Handle with care   N — Keep silence
O — Way in   P — Way out
Q — Beware of the traffic

Example: (E) 车辆慢行   (K) 远离草坪

Unit 6 Theme Parks

51. (   ) 当心车辆   (   ) 闲人免进
52. (   ) 入口   (   ) 禁止张贴
53. (   ) 会客时间   (   ) 请勿动手
54. (   ) 远离火种   (   ) 禁止吐痰
55. (   ) 免费入场   (   ) 小心轻放

Task 5

Directions: *The following is an advertisement. After reading it, you will find 3 questions or unfinished statements. For each question or statement there are 4 choices marked A, B, C and D. You should make the correct choice and mark the corresponding letter.*

56. How will people watch the game according to the advertisement?

   A. They will watch it on 50" Toshiba LED TV.

B. They will watch it on 6 HD flatscreens around the bar.

C. They will watch it in the office of Aviator Sports And Events Center.

D. They will watch it as soon as the tailgate party begins.

57. What can people enjoy throughout the game?

    A. Hot and cold food.

    B. Singing and dancing.

    C. Any food they like.

    D. Beer, wine and soda.

58. If you and your five friends will go to the party, how much should you pay for each person?

    A. $40.   B. $30.

    C. $50.   D. free.

Part Ⅳ Translation

Directions: *There are 5 sentences, numbered 61 through 65. Write your translation in the corresponding space.*

59. It's impossible to see and do everything in Walt Disney World, even in several days.

60. Theme parks tend to be much larger and more high-tech than the older amusement parks.

Unit 6 Theme Parks

61. In nineteen fifty-five, Walt Disney opened an entertainment park not far from Hollywood, California.

62. Actors dressed as Mickey walked around the park shaking hands with visitors.

63. Because Disney and his partner often saw mice running in and out of the old building where they worked, they decided to draw a cartoon mouse.

Part Ⅴ Writing

Directions: *Read the following telephone conversation and complete the telephone message below according to the content you read.*

说明：根据下面内容写一份电话留言

W: Good morning! Mr. Taylor's office. Can I help you?

M: Good morning! This is Sally Cook from Sunny Corporation. May I speak to Mr. Taylor?

W: I'm sorry. Mr. Taylor is occupied at the moment. May I take a message?

M: I'd like to see Mr. Taylor sometime next week. What about next Monday morning?

W: Oh, let me see... Sorry, Mr. Cook. Mr. Taylor has appointments the whole morning next Monday. Would Tuesday be all right?

M: Tuesday? No problem.

W: Then what time would be convenient for you?

73

M: Any time on Tuesday morning, I think.

W: Shall we say half past nine then?

M: Fine, thank you.

W: Thank you for your calling. Goodbye.

M: Goodbye.

Telephone Message

Date: Nov. 15   Time: 9:40

From: _____

To: _____

Message: _____

_____

_____

_____

_____

Signed by   Cindy

2017年6月高等学校英语应用能力考试(B级)

Part I Listening Comprehension (25 minutes)

Directions: This part is to test your listening ability. It consists of 4 sections.

Section A

Directions: This section is to test your ability to give proper responses. There are 7 recorded questions in it. After each question, there is a pause. The questions will be spoken **two times**. When you hear a question, you should decide on the correct answer from the 4 choices marked A, B, C and D given in your test paper. Then you should mark the center.

Example: You will hear:
You will read: A. I'm not sure.
B. You're right.
C. Yes, certainly.
D. That's interesting.

From the question we learn that the speaker is asking the listener to leave a message. Therefore, C. Yes, certainly is the correct answer. You should mark C. on the Answer Sheet with a single line through the center.

[A] [B] [C] [D]

Now the test will begin.

1. A. Let's have a break.   B. This way, please.
   C. Don't mention it.   D. No, thank you.
2. A. On Monday.   B. John Smith.
   C. Take it easy.   D. It's too late.
3. A. How do you do?   B. It doesn't matter.
   C. Yes, please.   D. Mind your step.
4. A. I'm afraid not.   B. Never mind.
   C. Hurry up.   D. Have a good time.
5. A. Go ahead, please.   B. Yes, I am.
   C. I'd love to.   D. He's from China.
6. A. Oh, I see.   B. Here it is.
   C. It's over there.   D. Yes, of course.
7. A. Go on, please.   B. Two dollars.
   C. Sure, I will.   D. Here you are.

Section B

Directions: This section is to test your ability to understand short dialogues. There are 7 recorded dialogues in it. After each dialogue, there is a recorded question. Both the dialogues and questions will be spoken **two times**. When you hear a question, you should decide on the correct answer from the 4 choices marked A, B, C and D given in your test paper. Then you should mark the corresponding letter on the Answer Sheet with a single line through the center. Now listen to the dialogues.

8. A. About 150 years ago.   B. About 120 years ago.
   C. About 115 years ago.   D. About 100 years ago.
9. A. Boring.   B. Difficult.
   C. Interesting.   D. Satisfactory.
10. A. Its location.   B. Its development.
    C. Its population.   D. Its history.
11. A. It is modern.   B. It is crowded.

C. It is small. D. It is quiet.

12. A. She is in poor health. B. She failed a test.
    C. She hasn't enough money. D. She hasn't got any offer.

13. A. Show his ID card. B. Fill in a form.
    C. Write a report. D. Pay some money.

14. A. She has her leg broken. B. She fell from a bicycle.
    C. She feels a back pain. D. She has got a headache.

Section C

Directions: *In this section, there are 2 recorded conversations. After each conversation, there are some recorded questions. Both the conversations and questions will be spoken **two times**. When you hear a question, you should decide on the correct answer from the 4 choices marked A, B, C and D given in your test paper. Then you should mark the corresponding letter on the Answer Sheet with a single line through the center. Now listen to the conversations.*

Conversation 1

15. A. An apartment with a good view.
    B. An apartment of two-bedrooms.
    C. An apartment on the ground floor.
    D. An apartment with central heating.

16. A. Near a subway station. B. Near a hotel.
    C. In the downtown. D. In the suburbs.

Conversation 2

17. A. To have better opportunities. B. To improve his skills.
    C. To work fewer hours. D. To get a higher salary.

18. A. For six years. B. For five years.
    C. For three years. D. For two years.

19. A. A professor. B. A manager.
    C. An engineer. D. A designer.

Section D

Directions: *In this section you will hear a recorded short passage. The passage is printed in the test paper, but with some words or phrases missing. The passage will be read* **three times**. *During the second reading, you are required to put the missing words or phrases on the Answer Sheet in order of the numbered blanks according to what you hear. The third reading is for you to check your writing. Now the passage will begin.*

First of all, on behalf of all the people from our company, I would like to say "Thank you for (20)_____ us to such a wonderful party". I think the music is (21)_____, the food and wine are very nice, and the people here are all very kind. Also we've enjoyed meeting and (22)_____ you, sharing the comfortable time together. We have really enjoyed ourselves. I hope we will be able to maintain the (23)_____ and make next year another great one together. Thank you again for the party. We've really had (24)_____.

Part Ⅱ Vocabulary & Structure (10 minutes)

Directions: *This part is to test your ability to construct correct and meaningful sentences. It consists of 2 sections.*

Section A

Directions: *In this section, there are 10 incomplete sentences. You are required to complete each one by deciding on the most appropriate word or words from the 4 choices marked A, B, C and D. Then you should mark the corresponding letter on the Answer Sheet with a single line through the center.*

25. It was not until yesterday _____ they decided to re-open the business talk.
    A. when   B. which   C. that   D. as

26. We have to _____ the cost of seeing up a new hospital in that area.

  A. work out B. put on C. fill up D. carry on

27. We need to _____ an eye on all the activities to make sure that people stay safe.

  A. catch B. keep C. take D. bring

28. The local government has always placed a strong emphasis _____ education and vocational training.

  A. with B. for C. on D. to

29. Don't take the wrong turn before you _____ the railway station.

  A. have B. run C. keep D. reach

30. The team doesn't mind _____ at weekends as long as they can finish the task.

  A. worked B. working C. to work D. work

31. We are a non-profit company _____ team members are from all over the country.

  A. whose B. that C. which D. what

32. The meeting room is so small that it can hold 20 people _____.

  A. at last B. at first C. at most D. at once

33. She gave us a detailed _____ of the local government's new health-care proposal.

  A. impression   B. explanation
  C. education   D. communication

34. Linda _____ her training in a joint company by the end of next month.

  A. finishes   B. has finished
  C. had finished   D. will have finished

Section B

Directions: *There are also 5 incomplete statements here. You should fill in each blank with the proper form of the word given in brackets. Write the word or words in the corresponding space on the Answer Sheet.*

35. We were impressed by the (suggest) _____ you made at yesterday's meeting.

36. The (long) _____ Charles has lived in this city, the more he likes it.
37. If you want to learn some terms related to your field, you will find this book might be (help) _____.
38. No one is allowed (smoke) _____ in public buildings according to the new regulation.
39. The new president (ask) _____ some tough questions by the reporter in the interview yesterday.

Part Ⅲ   Reading Comprehension (35 minutes)

Directions: *This part is to test your reading ability. There are 5 tasks for you to fulfill. You should read the reading materials carefully and do the tasks as you are instructed.*

Task 1

Directions: *After reading the following passage, you will find 5 questions or unfinished statements, numbered 40 to 44. For each question or statement, there are 4 choices marked A, B, C and D. You should make the correct choice and mark the corresponding letter on the Answer Sheet with a single line through the center.*

Notice of Baggage Inspection(检查)

To protect you and your fellow passengers, the Transportation Security Administration (TSA) is required by law to inspect all checked baggage. As part of this process, some bags are opened and inspected. Your bag was among those selected for inspection.

During the inspection, your bag and its contents may have been searched for prohibited(违禁的) items. After the inspection was completed, the contents were returned to your bag.

If the TSA security officer was unable to open your bag for inspection because it was locked, the officer may have been forced to break the locks on your bag. TSA sincerely regrets having to do this. However, TSA is not responsible for damage to your locks resulting from this necessary security measures.

For packing tips and suggestions on how to secure your baggage during your next trip, please visit: www.tsa.gov.

We appreciate your understanding and cooperation. If you have questions, comments, or concerns, please feel free to contact the TSA Contact Center.

40. According to the passage, TSA is required to inspect your baggage _____.
   A. with your written permission
   B. at the request of police
   C. by airlines
   D. by law

41. According to the Notice, the purpose of the inspection is to _____.
   A. find all overweight baggage
   B. search for prohibited items
   C. charge customs duties
   D. check damaged items

42. After the inspection, the contents in your bag would _____.
   A. be delivered to your address
   B. be given to you in person
   C. be returned to your bag
   D. be kept at the airport

43. If your bag is locked, the TSA security officer may have to _____.
   A. break the locks
   B. hand it over to police
   C. give up the inspection
   D. ask you to open the bag

44. If the locks of your bag are damaged because of the inspection, TSA will _____.
   A. pay for the damage
   B. buy you a new lock
   C. not be responsible for it
   D. not inspect it in your next trip

Task 2

Directions: *The following is a poster. After reading it, you will find 3 questions or unfinished statements, numbered 45 to 47. For each question or statement, there are 4 choices marked A, B, C and D. You should make the correct choice and mark the corresponding letter on the Answer Sheet with a single line through the center.*

Seymour Marine Discovery Center at Long Marine Lab

2017 DOCENT TRAINING

Applications due January 7, 2017!
JOIN OUR DOCENT TRAINNING PROGRAM AND
MAKE A DIFERENCE FOR THE OCEANS

Our dynamic 10-week education program beginning January 11, 2017 will give you all the tools you need to interpret innovative marine science and conservation to the public.

BECOME A VOLUNTEER

* Gain experience in public speaking
* Work with animals at the seawater table and shark pool
* interact with the Long Marine Lab community
* Participate in expanded and in-depth learning opportunities

APPLY NOW!

Applications are now being accepted and reviewed. To apply, download an application form at seymourcenter. ucsc. edu. Call (831) 459-3854 for more information. Summer availability is a must. Docents must be at least 18 years old by the start of training in January 2017.

The Seymour Center is dedicated to educating people about the role scientific research plays in the understanding and conservation of the world's oceans.

100 Shaffer Road, Santa Cruz. CA 95060
End of Delaware Avenue

45. How long does the docent training program last?

   A. Four weeks   B. Six weeks
   C. Eight weeks   D. Ten weeks

46. To apply for the program, you should _____.

   A. first download an application form
   B. be good at working with animals
   C. be an experienced public speaker
   D. first pay a visit to the lab

47. To attend the program, you must be at least _____.

   A. 14 years old   B. 16 years old
   C. 18 years old   D. 20 years old

Task 3

***Directions**: The following passage is about a survey conducted by Corvallis Clinic. After reading it, you should complete the information by filling in the blanks marked 48 to 52 (**in no more than 3 words**) in the table below. You should write your answers on the Answer Sheet correspondingly.*

Thank you for selecting the Corvallis Clinic (诊所) for your recent healthcare needs. To continue delivering the highest possible level of service, we survey our patients to learn about their experiences at our clinic. The comments and suggestions you provide about your visit will help us evaluate (评价) our services and improve our care.

This survey takes only a few minutes to complete. Your comments and suggestions are very important to us, and they will be kept confidential (保密). A postage-paid reply envelope is enclosed for your convenience. If you have any questions about this survey, please call our Service Center at 541-754-1374.

Thank you for helping us as we continually try our best to improve the quality of medical care. Please drop your completed survey in the mail as soon as possible.

Patient's Survey

Survey conducted by: Corvallis Clinic

Aim of the survey: to deliver the highest possible level of service

Values of patients comments and suggestions:

    1) helping to evaluate the clinic's (48)_____;

    2) helping to improve the clinic's (49)_____

Promise by the clinic: comments and suggestions to be kept (50)_____

Enclosure: a (51)_____ reply envelope

Contact: to call Service Center at (52)_____

Task 4

Directions: *The following is a list of terms used in Safety Management. After reading it, you are required to find the items equivalent to those given in Chinese in the table below. Then you should mark the corresponding letters in order of the numbered blanks, 53 through 57, on the Answer Sheet.*

- A — Warning equipment
- B — Accident management
- C — Protection measures
- D — Risk assessment
- E — Administrative controls
- F — Detection technique
- G — Failure analysis
- H — Responsible person
- I — Harmful substances
- J — Protection devices
- K — Accident statistics
- L — Safety standards
- M — Accident prevention
- N — Monitoring system
- O — Special operation
- P — Medical aid
- Q — Emergency rescue

Examples：(Q) 应急措施   (D) 风险评估

53. (　) 事故统计	(　) 检测技术
54. (　) 报警设备	(　) 医疗救护
55. (　) 有害物质	(　) 管理控制
56. (　) 保护措施	(　) 责任人
57. (　) 特殊作业	(　) 失效分析

Task 5

Directions：*Read the following passage. After reading it, you are required to complete the answers that follow the questions (No. 58 to No. 62). You should write your answers (in no more than 3 words) on the Answer Sheet correspondingly.*

ITaP Instructional Lab Etiquette（守则）

* This lab is a study zone—please limit your noise. Cell phones and other electronic communication devices should be turned off while inside the lab.
* Group studying—limit group studying to non-busy times. Gives chairs to others so they can use available computers.
* Log off from your computer—workstations left idle（空闲状态的）for more than 10 minutes will be reset to the log-in screen.
* Printouts are limited to 10-minute printing time—break large print jobs into smaller print jobs.
* Customer's forms or paper are not permitted in ITaP printers—this can damage the printers.
* Computers are available on a first-come-first-serve basis only during computer lab hours of operation and when no classes are scheduled in the room.

58. What should you do with your cell phones while you are inside the lab?

　　You should _____ your cell phones.

59. When can you do your group studying in the lab?

At _____ times.

60. Why should you break large print jobs into smaller ones?

    Because printouts are limited to _____ printing time.

61. Why are the customer's forms or paper not permitted in ITaP printers?

    They can _____ .

62. When can you use the computers in the lab?

    During the lab hours of _____ with no classes scheduled.

Part Ⅳ Translation — English into Chinese （25 minutes）

Directions：*This part, numbered 63 to 67, is to test your ability to translate English into Chinese. Each of the four sentences (No. 63 to No. 66) is followed by three choices of suggested translation marked A, B, and C. Make the best choice and write the corresponding letter on the Answer Sheet with a single line through the center. And then write your translation of the paragraph (No. 67) in the corresponding space on the Translation/Composition Sheet.*

63. The healthcare and social assistant sector will account for almost a third of the job growth from 2012 to 2022.

    A. 从 2012 年至 2022 年，从事医疗保健工作的员工将占社会救助业的三分之一。

    B. 从 2012 年至 2022 年，医疗保健和社会救助业几乎将占就业增长的三分之一。

    C. 从 2012 年至 2022 年，医疗保健和社会救助业将会占到三分之一的就业岗位。

64. Regardless of your line of work, sending business invitations will certainly be something you will face from time to time.

    A. 无论你从事哪个行业，发业务邀请函必然是你时不时要遇到的事情。

    B. 只要你从事这个业务，就摆脱不了需要经常去处理商务函电等事项。

    C. 不管从事的是哪一个行当，你经常要做的一件事情就是收发邀请函。

65. Our company makes a special effort to establish good communication and cooperative relationships between management and labor.

   A. 本公司重视与管理层和服务人员的沟通,建立了良好的合作关系。

   B. 本公司为已与我们建立良好贸易合作关系的客户提供特殊的服务。

   C. 本公司特别致力于建立管理层和员工之间良好的沟通与合作关系。

66. If you need any help in starting a business, our team will be right here for you.

   A. 如果你需要创业,我们团队就可以在此给你提供帮助。

   B. 你在创业中如需任何帮助,我们团队会随时为你提供。

   C. 如果你创业失败,我们团队将会帮助你重新制定计划。

67. Many items may be dangerous goods and could cause serious accidents when mailed. It is your responsibility to ensure that your parcel does not contain any dangerous goods. With your cooperation, accidents can be prevented. You could be held responsible if an accident occurred. If you wish to know whether you can mail a certain item, please call Customer Service at 1-800-267-1177.

_____
_____
_____
_____
_____
_____
_____
_____

Part V Writing (25 minutes)

Directions: This part is to test your ability to do practical writing. You are required to complete the Guest Experience Card according to the following information given in Chinese. Remember to do your writing on the Translation/Composition Sheet.

说明：假定你是张建林，根据所给内容填写下列顾客意见反馈表。

顾客姓名：张建林

顾客邮址：zhangjl999@163.com

抵达日期：2017年6月15日

抵达时间：上午11：30

内容：

  酒店员工非常友好，提供了良好的服务，尤其是一位叫John Chen的员工。

  酒店的房间干净整洁，餐厅的食物美味可口，住店的体验很不错。

  但是酒店离市中心较远，建议酒店增设从酒店到地铁站的班车（shuttle bus），为客人提供方便。

Guest Experience Card

We value your feedback

Name：(1)＿＿＿＿＿＿＿＿

Email address：(2)＿＿＿＿＿＿＿＿

Date of visit：(3)＿＿＿＿＿＿＿＿

Time of visit：(4)＿＿＿＿＿＿＿＿

Did our Team Members exceed your expectations? ＿Yes＿ If yes, please provide their names：(5)＿＿＿＿＿＿＿＿

Comments：

＿＿＿＿＿＿＿＿＿＿＿＿＿＿＿＿＿＿＿＿＿＿＿＿
＿＿＿＿＿＿＿＿＿＿＿＿＿＿＿＿＿＿＿＿＿＿＿＿
＿＿＿＿＿＿＿＿＿＿＿＿＿＿＿＿＿＿＿＿＿＿＿＿
＿＿＿＿＿＿＿＿＿＿＿＿＿＿＿＿＿＿＿＿＿＿＿＿

Thank you for choosing our hotel.

If you would like to talk to us about your experience today

Please contact the Guest Services Department at 1-888-601-1616

答案及听力材料

Key to Unit 1

Part Ⅰ Listening Comprehension

Section A

1～5 BCACD

Section B

6～10 CDCDA

Section C

11. introducers 12. necessary 13. politely 14. usually 15. It depends

Part Ⅱ Vocabulary & Structure

Section A

16～25 DABCD DCACD

Section B

26. working 27. suggestions 28. be repaired 29. more successful

30. creation 31. differences 32. friendly 33. birth 34. useful 35. medical

Part Ⅲ Reading Comprehension

Task 1

36～40 CACBD

Task 2

    41~45　AAADC

Task 3

    46. Bazaar　47. wholesale company　48. Japan

    49. the fashion industry　50. beauty products

Task 4

    51. E O　52. A F　53. I M　54. N C　55. B D

Task 5

    56. B　57. A　58. B

Part Ⅳ　Translation

（见课文译文）

Part Ⅴ　Writing

Sept. 20, 2016

Dear Miss Alice Washington,

    We would like to express our gratitude to you for your support and cooperation with us over the past years, and with great pleasure we would like to invite you to attend a dinner party to celebrate our company's tenth anniversary at Anhui Restaurant on September 24, 2016 (Saturday), at 7:00 p.m.

    We hope you have free time and attend the dinner party.

    Your early reply would be appreciated very much.

Yours sincerely,

Mike Kennedy

General Manager

Hefei Yuanyang Electronics Corporation

Script for Listening Comprehension

Part Ⅰ　Listening Comprehension

Directions: This part consists of 3 sections.

答案及听力材料

Section A

Directions: *There are 5 recorded questions in it. After each question, there is a pause. The questions will be spoken two times. When you hear a question, you should decide on the correct answer from the 4 choices marked A, B, C and D. Then you should mark your choice.*

1. Hello, Tom. Can you introduce me to that man?
2. Haven't we met somewhere?
3. I wonder if I could meet the director with a pair of sunglasses.
4. Hi, please allow me to introduce myself. I'm John from Microsoft.
5. What's your plan for this weekend?

Section B

Directions: *There are 5 recorded dialogues in it. After each dialogue, there is a recorded question. The dialogues and questions will be spoken only once. When you hear a question, you should decide on the correct answer from the 4 choices marked A, B, C and D. Then you should mark your choice.*

6. M: Is it still raining?
   W: Yes. And the wind is blowing.
   Q: What is the weather like?

7. W: Should I get some more typing paper for you?
   M: Please do. We've almost run out of it.
   Q: What will the woman do?

8. W: Help yourself to a cigarette.
   M: No, thanks. I've already given it up.
   Q: What do you know about the man?

9. W: Have you ever been to Canada?
   M: Not yet. But I hope to go there one day.
   Q: What do we know from the dialogue?

10. M: How was your interview?
    W: Very successful. The employer seemed very interested in me.
    Q: How did the woman feel about the interview?

Section C

Directions: *In this section you will hear a recorded short passage. The passage will be read three times. During the second reading, you are required to fill in the missing words or phrases according to what you hear. The third reading is for you to check your writing. Now the passage will begin.*

When a person wants to know someone, he often does so through others' introduction, but in some circumstances, there are no (11) <u>introducers</u>, and then self-introduction, which can be very simple, becomes (12) <u>necessary</u>. You only have to walk up to the one you want to meet, say "Hello!" to him (13) <u>politely</u>, tell him your name and introduce yourself briefly. Then the one you are speaking to will (14) <u>usually</u> react to your introduction in a polite way. Of course, there are formal and informal forms of self-introduction. Which one shall we choose? (15) <u>It depends</u>. If the two have different social status (社会地位), the formal form should be used.

Key to Unit 2

Part Ⅰ   Listening Comprehension

Section A

　　1~5　BADDC

Section B

　　6~10　CADBD

Section C

　　11. most important   12. rain   13. winter   14. The animals   15. milk

Part Ⅱ   Vocabulary & Structure

Section A

　　16~25　ACCDC　CCBAD

Section B

　　26. difficulty   27. appearance   28. quickly   29. natural   30. faster
　　31. had lived   32. driving   33. effective   34. communication   35. impossible

答案及听力材料

Part Ⅲ Reading Comprehension

Task 1

36~40 BCBAD

Task 2

41~45 DADBB

Task 3

46. clean   47. easy to use   48. reduced   49. each station   50. 5

Task 4

51. L I   52. G E   53. A O   54. H C   55. K J

Task 5

56. B   57. B   58. D

Part Ⅳ Translation

（见课文译文）

Part Ⅴ Writing

Malaysia Visa Application Form
Full name <u>Laurel Lombard</u>
Date of birth <u>Feb. 12. 1988</u>
Gender <u>female</u>   Marital status <u>single</u>
Citizenship <u>American</u>   Citizenship at birth <u>American</u>
Permanent address <u>No. 12 Skyscraper Street，New York, N. Y. 12311, U. S. A.</u>
Present address <u>the same as above</u>
Occupation <u>Office Director of Amazing Legend Company</u>
Reason for visit <u>travelling</u>
Proposed duration of stay <u>4 days</u>
Signature *Laurel Lombard*   Date <u>Sept. 20, 2016</u>

Script for Listening Comprehension

Part Ⅰ Listening Comprehension

Directions: *This part consists of 3 sections.*

Section A

Directions: *There are 5 recorded questions in it. After each question, there is a pause. The questions will be spoken two times. When you hear a question, you should decide on the correct answer from the 4 choices marked A, B, C and D. Then you should mark your choice.*

1. Are you Mr. Baker from America?
2. How do you like your work?
3. Would you please give me the report, Tom?
4. What's your father's job?
5. Would you like a cup of coffee?

Section B

Directions: *There are 5 recorded dialogues in it. After each dialogue, there is a recorded question. The dialogues and questions will be spoken only once. When you hear a question, you should decide on the correct answer from the 4 choices marked A, B, C and D. Then you should mark your choice.*

6. W: What can I do for you, sir?

   M: Well, I want to buy a T-shirt.

   Q: What does the man want to buy?

7. M: What's your plan for the summer holiday?

   W: I'm going to Australia.

   Q: What's the woman going to do for the summer holiday?

8. W: May I use this telephone?

   M: Sorry, it doesn't work.

   Q: What does the woman want to do?

9. M: Excuse me, where is the manager's office?

   W: It's on the second floor.

Q: On which floor is the manager's office?

10. W: May I have a double room for tonight?

M: Sorry, there're only single rooms available.

Q: Where does the conversation take place?

Section C

Directions: *In this section you will hear a recorded short passage. The passage will be read three times. During the second reading, you are required to fill in the missing words or phrases according to what you hear. The third reading is for you to check your writing. Now the passage will begin.*

Britain does not grow rice. The summer is not hot enough. The (11) most important crop in Britain is wheat. Wheat and other crops grow best in the east of Britain. In the west there is a lot of highland and a lot of (12) rain . Here grass grows well. So, in the west of Britain, most farms are animal farms. They are not crop farms. The British (13) winter is mild and the grass grows all the year. (14) The animals live out in the fields and on the highlands. The British people eat a lot of meat and they drink a lot of (15) milk.

Key to Unit 3

Part Ⅰ　Listening Comprehension

Section A

1~5　BBACA

Section B

6~10　BCDBB

Section C

11. moving　12. increase　13. as fast as　14. carrying　15. any change

Part Ⅱ　Vocabulary & Structure

Section A

16~25　CDACA　ACCAD

Section B

26. selfish　27. invention　28. expression　29. decision　30. explanation

31. application   32. swimming   33. development   34. lucky   35. widely

Part Ⅲ   Reading Comprehension

Task 1

36～40   BDCAC

Task 2

41～45   BDCAD

Task 3

46. management   47. communication skills   48. leadership

49. a sales manager   50. (317) 555-0118

Task 4

51. P N   52. J L   53. H D   54. A G   55. C B

Task 5

56. A   57. C   58. A

Part Ⅳ   Translation

（见课文译文）

Part Ⅴ   Writing

Dec. 26, 2016

Dear Vincent Freund,

Thank you and your family for offering me the opportunity to celebrate Christmas Even with you this year.

This is the first time I have ever had the chance to spend Christmas Eve with a Western family. It was really fantastic and unforgettable!

I'll remember this Christmas Eve, and, above all, the hospitality you and your family showed me.

Thank you again, and wish you best wishes in the coming new year.

Jack Chen

答案及听力材料

Script for Listening Comprehension

Part I Listening Comprehension

Directions: This part consists of 3 sections.

Section A

Directions: There are 5 recorded questions in it. After each question, there is a pause. The questions will be spoken two times. When you hear a question, you should decide on the correct answer from the 4 choices marked A, B, C and D. Then you should mark your choice.

1. Have you read the author's latest bestseller?
2. I'm from Thailand. What about you?
3. Carol lives near here, doesn't she?
4. How is Mary feeling today?
5. Excuse me. Where can I find the apartment manager?

Section B

Directions: There are 5 recorded dialogues in it. After each dialogue, there is a recorded question. The dialogues and questions will be spoken only once. When you hear a question, you should decide on the correct answer from the 4 choices marked A, B, C and D. Then you should mark your choice.

6. M: Shall we make another pot of coffee?

    W: Why not?

    Q: What does the man mean?

7. M: I don't know if I should take the early or late bus.

    W: Does it matter? You don't need to be back until midnight.

    Q: What does the woman say about the bus?

8. M: I'd like to apply for the position you advertised in the paper.

    W: A good knowledge of English and French is the must.

    Q: What does the woman mean?

9. W: Has the city airport ever been closed because of the fog?

    M: Only a couple of times.

    Q: What does the man say about the airport?

10. W: I think I'll take the half-day tour of the city.

M: Why not the whole day?

Q: What does the man suggest that the woman do?

Section C

Directions: *In this section you will hear a recorded short passage. The passage will be read three times. During the second reading, you are required to fill in the missing words or phrases according to what you hear. The third reading is for you to check your writing. Now the passage will begin.*

We cannot feel speed. But our senses let us know that we are (11) moving. We see things moving past us and feel that we are being shaken. We can feel acceleration, an (12) increase in speed. But we notice it for only a short time. For instance, we feel it during the take-off run of an airliner. We feel the plane's acceleration because our bodies do not gain speed (13) as fast as the plane does. It seems that something is pushing us back against the seat. Actually, our bodies are trying to stay in the same plane while the plane is (14) carrying us forward. Soon the plane reaches a steady speed. Then, because there is no longer (15) any change in speed, the feeling of forward motion stops.

Key to Unit 4

Part Ⅰ Listening Comprehension

Section A

1～5 ADABC

Section B

6～10 ACACD

Section C

11. introduce   12. sell   13. North America   14. customers

15. look forward to

Part Ⅱ Vocabulary & Structure

Section A

16～25 BABBA   CBAAA

Section B

26. interested   27. wonderful   28. organization   29. immediately

答案及听力材料

30. emailed   31. communication   32. growth   33. will meet

34. payment   35. service

Part Ⅲ   Reading Comprehension

Task 1

36~40 CBCAC

Task 2

41~45 CBCCC

Task 3

46. knowledge   47. a vegetable   48. used tea leaves

49. milk   50. Tea-time

Task 4

51. C Q   52. O J   53. P K   54. B F   55. I E

Task 5

56. B   57. C   58. D

Part Ⅳ   Translation

（见课文译文）

Part Ⅴ   Writing

To：groupsales@aston.com
From：foxworthy@126.com
Subject：reservation
Date：Dec. 20, 2016
Dear Sir or Madam, I would like to make a reservation of four rooms: one single room and three double rooms. In addition, I would like to rent a conference room on the afternoon of December 26th, used for business talks. Please email me your reply as soon as possible, and tell me whether you have vacancies, the prices of the rooms, as well as whether I should pay a deposite in advance. Yours sincerely, Tammy Foxworthy

Script for Listening Comprehension

Part Ⅰ Listening Comprehension

Directions: *This part consists of 3 sections.*

Section A

Directions: *There are 5 recorded questions in it. After each question, there is a pause. The questions will be spoken two times. When you hear a question, you should decide on the correct answer from the 4 choices marked A, B, C and D. Then you should mark your choice.*

1. Excuse me. May I see your boss now?
2. When is the manager leaving?
3. Can I help you with your luggage, sir?
4. Have you ever been to the United States?
5. What do you think of our sales plan?

Section B

Directions: *There are 5 recorded dialogues in it. After each dialogue, there is a recorded question. The dialogues and questions will be spoken only once. When you hear a question, you should decide on the correct answer from the 4 choices marked A, B, C and D. Then you should mark your choice.*

6. W: What's the matter with you, Peter?
   M: I've got a headache.
   Q: What's Peter's problem?

7. M: Excuse me. Would you mind if I use your telephone?
   W: Not at all. It's over there on the table.
   Q: What does the man want to do?

8. W: Hello. ABC Company. Can I help you?
   M: Yes. I'd like to talk to your sales manager.
   Q: Whom does the man want to speak to?

9. M: Please show me your driver's license, Madam.
   W: What's the problem, officer?
   Q: What's the possible relationship between them?

答案及听力材料

10. W: What kind of room do you want to book, sir?

M: I'd like to book a single room with bath.

Q: What is the man doing?

Section C

Directions: *In this section you will hear a recorded short passage. The passage will be read three times. During the second reading, you are required to fill in the missing words or phrases according to what you hear. The third reading is for you to check your writing. Now the passage will begin.*

Ladies and gentlemen,

It's a great pleasure to have you visit us today. I'm very happy to have the opportunity to (11) introduce our company to you.

The company was established in 1950. We mainly manufacture electronic goods and (12) sell them all over the world. Our sales were about $100 million last year and our business is growing steadily.

We have offices in Asia, (13) North America and Europe. We have about 1,000 employees who are actively working to serve the needs of our (14) customers. In order to further develop our overseas market, we need your help to promote (促销) our products.

I (15) look forward to doing business with all of you. Thank you.

Key to Unit 5

Part I Listening Comprehension

Section A

1~5 BADCA

Section B

6~10 DADAD

Section C

11. show   12. factory   13. just a year ago   14. do our best

15. have a good time

Part Ⅱ Vocabulary & Structure

Section A

16～25   BACAA   CACAB

Section B

26. attractive   27. impolite   28. complaint   29. disappointed

30. exciting   31. carelessness   32. brought   33. driving

34. effectively   35. had followed

Part Ⅲ Reading Comprehension

Task 1

36～40   ACDBD

Task 2

41～45   ADDBA

Task 3

46. apples   47. little spots   48. a reduced price

49. a credit   50. the right quality

Task 4

51. B N   52. H J   53. I G   54. F E   55. A L

Task 5

56. D   57. A   58. B

Part Ⅳ Translation

（见课文译文）

Part Ⅴ Writing

Nov. 13th, 2016

Dear Sir or Madam:

　　I am very interested in the position of English tourist guide you advertised in "Xin'an Evening" of Nov. 13th, 2016. Your kind consideration of my application would be appreciated.

I studied at Huainan Vocational College from September 2013 through June 2016. During the three school years I studied hard, and worked as part-time tourist guide in my spare time. So I am confident that I am qualified for the job I am applying for.

Hope you will give me the chance to attend the interview and show my ability. My mobilephone number is 15818845666. You can contact me at your convenience.

Yours faithfully,
RongZhi

Script for Listening Comprehension

Part I Listening Comprehension

Directions: *This part consists of 3 sections.*

Section A

Directions: *There are 5 recorded questions in it. After each question, there is a pause. The questions will be spoken two times. When you hear a question, you should decide on the correct answer from the 4 choices marked A, B, C and D. Then you should mark your choice.*

1. Lovely day, isn't it?
2. I'm planning to go to Paris. Have you ever been there?
3. I'm not satisfied with your service. I want to speak to your manager.
4. Would you like a cup of coffee? I just made some.
5. Well, I hate to complain, but this delay has caused me to miss my meeting.

Section B

Directions: *There are 5 recorded dialogues in it. After each dialogue, there is a recorded question. The dialogues and questions will be spoken only once. When you hear a question, you should decide on the correct answer from the 4 choices marked A, B, C and D. Then you should mark your choice.*

6. M: Jane, what about going to the concert tonight?

   W: Oh, I'm sorry, Tom. I'm tired today.

   Q: What will the woman probably do tonight?

7. W: The shirt is thirty-nine dollars, sir.

   M: All right, I'll take it.

   Q: What is the relationship between the two speakers?

8. M: Why didn't you come to the class yesterday, Helen?

   W: Oh, my mother was ill, and I had to take her to hospital.

   Q: Why didn't Helen go to school yesterday?

9. M: My flight leaves at 4:30.

   W: Then you'd better leave for the airport at half past two.

   Q: What can we learn from this conversation?

10. M: Excuse me, could you tell me how to go to the Bank of China?

    W: Go along Rose Street, turn right at the next corner and there you are.

    Q: Where is the Bank of China?

Section C

Directions: *In this section you will hear a recorded short passage. The passage will be read three times. During the second reading, you are required to fill in the missing words or phrases according to what you hear. The third reading is for you to check your writing. Now the passage will begin.*

Ladies and Gentlemen,

Welcome to you all. We are pleased to have you here to visit our company.

Today, we will first (11) <u>show</u> you around our company, and then you will go and see our (12) <u>factory</u> and research center. The research center was built (13) <u>just a year ago</u>.

You may ask any questions you have during the visit. We will (14) <u>do our best</u> to make your visit comfortable and worthwhile.

Again, I would like to extend a warmest welcome to all of you on behalf of our company, and I hope that you will enjoy your stay here and (15) <u>have a good time</u>.

Key to Unit 6

Part Ⅰ Listening Comprehension

Section A

1~5 BACDC

答案及听力材料

Section B

6~10 ADCBC

Section C

11. degree   12. other kinds   13. training class   14. work   15. better

Part Ⅱ   Vocabulary & Structure

Section A

16~25 ABCDD   DCDCB

Section B

26. helpful   27. better   28. combination   29. development   30. had come

31. best   32. talking   33. natural   34. dead   35. to live

Part Ⅲ   Reading Comprehension

Task 1

36~40 BCABD

Task 2

41~45 CBCCD

Task 3

46. Tourist Information Centre   47. local events   48. local coach companies

49. walking tours   50. guidebooks

Task 4

51. Q D   52. O I   53. J L   54. B H   55. A M

Task 5

56. B   57. D   58. B

Part Ⅳ   Translation

(见课文译文)

Part Ⅴ Writing

Telephone Message

Date: <u>Nov. 15</u>   Time: <u>9:40</u>

From: <u>Sally Cook</u>

To: <u>Mr. Taylor</u>

Message: <u>Ms. Sally Cook of Sunny Corporation telephoned to say that she would like to see you Tuesday next week, at 9:30 a.m.</u>

Signed by <u>Cindy</u>

Script for Listening Comprehension

Part Ⅰ Listening Comprehension

Directions: *This part consists of 3 sections.*

Section A

Directions: *There are 5 recorded questions in it. After each question, there is a pause. The questions will be spoken two times. When you hear a question, you should decide on the correct answer from the 4 choices marked A, B, C and D. Then you should mark your choice.*

1. It's a fine day. Why not go to the zoo?
2. When can I take my winter vacation?
3. Did you enjoy the performance last night?
4. Can we have dinner together this weekend?
5. Professor Smith, may I ask you a few questions?

Section B

Directions: *There are 5 recorded dialogues in it. After each dialogue, there is a recorded question. The dialogues and questions will be spoken only once. When you hear a question, you should decide on the correct answer from the 4 choices*

答案及听力材料

marked A, B, C and D. Then you should mark your choice.

6. M: I prefer coffee to tea. What about you, Jane?

   W: Just water.

   Q: What will the woman like to have?

7. W: Excuse me. Can you call a taxi for me?

   M: Sorry. The telephone is out of order.

   Q: What does the man mean?

8. M: What's wrong with me, doctor?

   W: Just a cold. Nothing serious.

   Q: What's the probable relationship between the two speakers?

9. M: Don't you usually drive to work?

   W: No. I walk to work every day.

   Q: How does the woman usually go to work?

10. M: My computer doesn't work.

    W: Why don't you have it repaired?

    Q: What does the woman think the man should do?

Section C

Directions: *In this section you will hear a recorded short passage. The passage will be read three times. During the second reading, you are required to fill in the missing words or phrases according to what you hear. The third reading is for you to check your writing. Now the passage will begin.*

Today more and more people begin to understand that study does not come to an end with school graduation. Education is not just a college (11) degree; it is life itself. Many people are not interested in studying at a college, and they are interested in (12) other kinds of learning. They may go to a (13) training class in their own field; they may improve their (14) work skills by following television courses. They certainly know that if they know more or learn more, they can get (15) better jobs or earn more money.

2017年6月高等学校英语应用能力考试(B级)答案

Part Ⅰ　Listening Comprehension（每题1分，共24分）

Section A

1. D　2. B　3. C　4. A　5. B　6. D　7. C

Section B

8. A　9. D　10. C　11. A　12. C　13. B　14. D

Section C

15. B　16. C　17. A　18. B　19. C

Section D

20. inviting　21. lovely　22. talking to　23. good relationship
24. a great time

Part Ⅱ　Vocabulary & Structure（每题1分，共15分）

Section A

25～29. CABCD　　30～34. BACBD

Section B

35. suggestion　36. longer　37. helpful　38. to smoke　39. was asked

Part Ⅲ　Reading Comprehension（40—47各2分，48—62各1分，共31分）

Task 1

40～44. DBCAC

Task 2

45. D　46. A　47. C

Task 3

48. services　49. care　50. confidential　51. postage-paid
52. 541-754-1374

Task 4

53. KF　54. AP　55. IE　56. CH　57. OG

Task 5

58. turn off　59. non-busy　60. 10-minute　61. damage the printer

答案及听力材料

62. operation

Part Ⅳ　Translation—English into Chinese（63—66 的评分有 3 个等级，
　　　　　分值分别是 2—1—0；67 题的分值为 7 分。总分 15）

63. B-C-A　　64. A-C-B　　65. C-A-B　　66. B-A-C

67. 很多物品具有危险性，邮寄中可能会造成严重事故。确保所寄包裹不含危险品是您应尽的责任。您的合作会有助于防止事故发生。如果确有事故发生，您将承担责任。对是否可以邮寄某些物品想有更多了解，请拨打 1-800-267-1177，致电客服中心。

Part Ⅴ　Writing（共 15 分）

（1）Zhang Jianlin

（2）zhangjl1999@163.com

（3）June 15, 2017

（4）11:30 a.m.

（5）John Chen

Your staff members are very friendly. They served me perfectly well. Among them, the outstanding is John Chen.

Also, I must say that all your rooms are clean and tidy. Your food is very delicious. I did have a wonderful experience at your hotel.

But it is also true that your hotel is a little far from the downtown. So, I suggest that there be shuttle buses between your hotel and the subway station, which will provide the guests with more convenience.

Script for Listening Comprehension

Part Ⅰ　Listening Comprehension　(25 minutes)

Directions: *This part is to test your listening ability. It consists of 4 sections.*

Section A

Directions: *This section is to test your ability to give proper responses. There are 7 recorded questions in it. After each question, there is a pause. The ques-*

tions will be spoken two times. When you hear a question, you should decide on the correct answer from the 4 choices marked A, B, C and D given in your test paper. Then you should mark the corresponding letter on the Answer Sheet with a single line through the center.

Example: You will hear: Mr. Smith is not in. Could you please give him a message?

You will read: A. I'm not sure.

B. You're right.

C. Yes, certainly.

D. That's interesting.

From the question we learn that the speaker is asking the listener to leave a message. Therefore, C. Yes, certainly *is the correct answer. You should mark C on the Answer Sheet with a single line through the center. Now the test will begin.*

1. Can I help you, madam?

2. May I have your name, please?

3. Would you like a cup of coffee?

4. Shall we meet on Friday?

5. Excuse me. Are you Jane Smith from England?

6. Are you interested in this training course?

7. Would you like to attend the sales meeting?

Section B

Directions: This section is to test your ability to understand short dialogues. There are 7 recorded dialogues in it. After each dialogue, there is a recorded question. Both the dialogues and questions will be spoken two times. When you hear a question, you should decide on the correct answer from the 4 choices marked A, B, C and D given in your test paper. Then you should mark the corresponding letter on the Answer Sheet with a single line through the center. Now listen to the dialogues.

8. M: This building looks quite old.

W: Yes, it was built about 150 years ago.

Q: When was the building built?

9. W: Are you satisfied with your job?

M: Yes, the boss is nice and the pay is good.

答案及听力材料

   Q: What does the man think of his job?

10. W: Does your city have a large population?

    M: Yes, about 3 million people.

    Q: What does the woman ask about the city?

11. M: Have you ever been to Shenzhen?

    W: Yes, many times. It's a very modern city.

    Q: What does the woman think of the city?

12. M: Are you planning to study abroad?

    W: I wish I could. But I haven't got enough money.

    Q: What problem does the woman have?

13. M: Excuse me. How can I apply for a membership card?

    W: Please fill in this form first.

    Q: What will the man probably do first?

14. M: Hi, Jane. What's wrong with you?

    W: I've got a headache.

    Q: What can we learn about the woman?

Section C

Directions: In this section, there are 2 recorded conversations. After each conversation, there are some recorded questions. Both the conversations and questions will be spoken two times. When you hear a question, you should decide on the correct answer from the 4 choices marked A, B, C and D given in your test paper. Then you should mark the corresponding letter on the Answer Sheet with a single line through the center. Now listen to the conversations.

Conversation 1

W: Good morning.

M: Good morning. I want to rent an apartment.

W: What kind of apartment do you want?

M: A two-bedroom one.

W: Where do you want it to be?

M: Near my office in the downtown.

W: Yes. We have several apartments available.

15. What kind of apartment does the man want to rent?

16. Where does the man want the apartment to be?

Conversation 2

W: Good morning.

M: Good morning.

W: Why are you interested in this job?

M: I want to have more opportunities.

W: Good. How long have you been working at your current position?

M: For five years.

W: What do you expect to be in a few years?

M: I hope I can become a skilled engineer.

17. Why does the man apply for the job?

18. How long has the man been working in his current position?

19. What does the man expect to be in the near future?

Section D

Directions: *In this section you will hear a recorded short passage. The passage is printed in the test paper, but with some words or phrases missing. The passage will be read three times. During the second reading, you are required to put the missing words or phrases on the Answer Sheet in order of the numbered blanks according to what you hear. The third reading is for you to check your writing. Now the passage will begin.*

First of all, on behalf of all the people from our company, I would like to say "Thank you for (20) inviting us to such a wonderful party". I think the music is (21) lovely, the food and wine are very nice, and the people here are all very kind. Also we've enjoyed meeting and (22) talking to you, sharing the comfortable time together. We have really enjoyed ourselves. I hope we will be able to maintain the (23) good relationship and make next year another great one together. Thank you again for the party. We've really had (24) a great time.